Winning by Not Engaging: Responding to a US Trade War

Vanida Plamondon

WINNING BY NOT ENGAGING: RESPONDING TO A US TRADE WAR

First edition. December 12, 2024.

ISBN: 979-8230620716

Written by Vanida Plamondon.

Canada's Trade War Disadvantage

When it comes to trade wars, especially with the United States, Canada is at a clear disadvantage. The economies are simply not on equal footing. The US has the leverage of size and power, and when they throw their weight around with tariffs and restrictions, they can absorb the economic fallout much better than we can. Trying to fight fire with fire doesn't work when your fire is a small campfire and theirs is a wildfire. Retaliating with tariffs and restrictions of our own just ends up hurting Canadians more than it hurts anyone south of the border. Instead of wasting time and resources on that kind of response, we need a plan that doesn't play by their rules.

We have to think about what we can control. Tariffs are designed to make us panic, to create instability in our economy, and to turn up the pressure on our leaders to react. If we don't take the bait, we're already ahead. Canada should focus on shoring up its own economy so that when the US tries these bullying tactics, they don't hit as hard. Protecting Canadian industries from the impact of US tariffs doesn't mean we have to escalate the fight. It means we use our resources to support our own businesses and workers, so they can weather the storm.

One of the biggest vulnerabilities we face is the affordability crisis. The rising cost of living in Canada isn't just a day-to-day burden for people; it's a weak spot that makes any economic disruption hit that much harder. When people are already stretched thin, things like higher prices for goods due to tariffs can push them over the edge. Addressing the affordability crisis isn't just about making life better for Canadians; it's about creating a buffer that protects them when external shocks, like a trade war, come along.

We've talked before about how meaningful, evidence-based policies can tackle affordability. Building affordable housing, making essentials like food and energy more accessible, and supporting small businesses can all make a huge difference. Imagine if, instead of scrambling to deal with the fallout of US tariffs, we had systems in place that made those tariffs less effective. If Canadians could rely on affordable housing, reasonable grocery bills, and steady jobs, the pressure from a trade war wouldn't hit as hard. The US could throw everything they've got at us, and we'd still be standing.

This kind of preparation doesn't just help in a trade war; it's good policy, period. By addressing affordability now, we're not just solving today's problems. We're making sure Canadians are better protected from whatever comes next. A strong, resilient economy isn't built on reacting to threats; it's built on being ready for them. Canada's leaders have a choice. They can keep reacting, or they can start preparing. That's how we win—not by fighting, but by refusing to lose.

History Of Canada-US Trade Relations

The trade relationship between Canada and the United States has always been complicated. We're each other's biggest trading partners, which sounds great on paper, but it comes with its share of headaches. The North American Free Trade Agreement, or NAFTA, was supposed to smooth out some of those bumps when it came into force in 1994. It created one of the largest free-trade zones in the world, including Mexico, and was designed to boost economic growth and make trade easier. For Canada, it opened up opportunities in sectors like manufacturing, agriculture, and energy by reducing or eliminating tariffs. At the same time, though, it came with a few catches. The US is a tough neighbour to deal with, and they've always been quick to flex their economic muscle when it suits them.

NAFTA worked reasonably well for a couple of decades, but it was never without its critics. Some industries in Canada felt the heat, especially manufacturing, as jobs moved to places like Mexico where labour costs were lower. There was also the softwood lumber dispute, which has been a thorn in the side of Canada-US trade for what feels like forever. Even with NAFTA in place, the US kept imposing tariffs on Canadian lumber, claiming unfair subsidies. Canada would win disputes in trade courts, but the US would find ways to drag it out or ignore the rulings. It's a classic example of how trade agreements don't always prevent disputes when one side decides to play dirty.

Fast forward to 2018, and NAFTA was replaced by the United States-Mexico-Canada Agreement, or USMCA. It wasn't a complete overhaul, but it did make some changes. The US wanted to tweak the deal to protect its own interests. For example, they pushed for stricter rules on auto manufacturing and got concessions on dairy products, which put more pressure on Canadian farmers. It wasn't a perfect deal for Canada, but with the US threatening to pull out of NAFTA altogether, there wasn't much choice but to negotiate. The USMCA was about damage control more than anything else.

Then there are the trade disputes that keep popping up. Softwood lumber is still a sore spot, but it's not the only one. Aluminum and steel tariffs made headlines a few years back when the US slapped duties on Canadian exports, claiming national security concerns. It was a ridiculous excuse, but it still hurt Canadian businesses. Canada retaliated with tariffs of its own, targeting everything from US steel to Kentucky bourbon. It was a messy situation, and while things eventually settled down, it left a bitter taste.

The problem with Canada-US trade is that even when we have agreements in place, they don't guarantee smooth sailing. The US is quick to put its own interests first, and Canada often ends up in the position of having to defend itself. It's a relationship built on necessity more than trust, and that's why these disputes keep happening. Whether it's softwood lumber, dairy, or aluminum, the US knows it holds most of the cards and isn't shy about using them.

Canada, Western Nations, And Globalization

Historically, western nations, including Canada, built their economic strength on the backs of vulnerable nations. It's an uncomfortable truth, but it's one we have to face. Colonization and resource extraction are at the heart of that story, where wealth was funnelled from poorer regions to enrich already powerful countries. This was often done under the guise of trade or development, but the reality was exploitation. Whether it was mining in Africa, agriculture in South America, or manufacturing in Asia, the global system was designed to keep certain nations at the top while others provided the labour and resources.

That system is starting to shift. Many of the countries that were once considered easy targets for exploitation are finding ways to break free from those dynamics. They've invested in their own industries, built stronger economies, and are demanding a fairer share of the global wealth. Nations like China, India, and Brazil are no longer content to be treated as second-class players on the world stage. Others are following suit, and globalization is evolving in ways that are making it harder for western countries to maintain their grip.

For Canada, this presents a new challenge. As the pool of vulnerable nations shrinks, there's a risk that the spotlight turns inward. If wealthier western countries can no longer exploit the same overseas resources and labour they once did, they might start looking for opportunities closer to home. Canada's economy, with its resource-heavy foundation and reliance on trade, could make it a target. This is especially concerning when you consider the growing wealth disparity and income inequality within Canada itself. A nation with deep economic divides is easier to exploit because its citizens are less likely to have the collective power to resist.

We've seen what happens when wealth and power concentrate at the top. The average person becomes more vulnerable to policies and trade deals that benefit only a select few. In Canada, the growing gap between the rich and everyone else creates a weak spot. It means less resilience in the face of economic shocks, whether those come from external trade pressures or internal mismanagement. If the majority of Canadians are struggling to make ends meet, it's much harder to push back against policies that could sell out the nation's interests for short-term gains.

What makes this even more pressing is the way other western countries have shown they're willing to exploit each other when it suits them. Trade disputes among allies have become more common, and economic alliances can crumble when self-interest takes over. Canada's position as a middle power doesn't offer much protection. Without strong economic safeguards and a population that's empowered to demand better, it's not hard to imagine a scenario where Canada becomes the next weak link in the chain.

Addressing this vulnerability starts at home. Reducing wealth disparity and giving Canadians more economic stability isn't just a matter of fairness; it's a matter of survival. If Canada wants to protect itself from being exploited, whether by external powers or even by its own elites, it has to make sure its citizens are in a position to stand up for their rights. An economy built on inequality is an economy built on shaky ground. And in a world where the rules are always shifting, shaky ground is the last thing Canada can afford.

Economic Impacts Of Trade Wars

Trade wars are bad news for just about everyone. When tariffs are introduced, they act as a tax on imported goods, and that cost doesn't just vanish into thin air. It gets passed along, and it's the businesses and consumers who end up footing the bill. The idea behind tariffs is to protect domestic industries by making foreign goods more expensive. On paper, it sounds like a way to give local businesses a competitive edge, but in reality, it creates a ripple effect that hits economies hard.

For businesses, tariffs mean higher input costs. Many industries rely on imported materials and components to produce their goods. Take aluminum and steel as an example. When tariffs were slapped on these materials, companies that depend on them for manufacturing, like carmakers or appliance producers, saw their costs go up. They either had to absorb those costs, which cuts into their profits, or pass them on to consumers, which risks driving customers away. Neither option is good for business. Small and medium-sized enterprises feel this pinch even more because they don't have the same financial cushion or bargaining power as larger corporations.

Consumers don't escape unscathed either. Higher costs for businesses almost always translate into higher prices at the checkout. Tariffs on everyday items, from food to electronics, mean people have to stretch their budgets further. For lower-income families, who already spend a larger share of their income on essentials, this is especially painful. It creates a situation where the very people who can least afford it bear the brunt of these trade policies.

Tariffs also disrupt supply chains. In today's interconnected world, goods often cross multiple borders before reaching their final destination. A tariff at any point in that chain can cause delays and increase costs. Businesses are forced to find alternative suppliers or routes, which takes time and money. This kind of uncertainty makes it harder for companies to plan and invest, slowing down economic growth.

There's also a psychological impact. When a trade war escalates, it creates instability in markets. Businesses start holding back on spending, hiring, and expansion because they don't know what's coming next. Investors get skittish, and consumer confidence takes a hit. People worry about rising prices, job security, and the overall economy. This fear can be just as damaging as the tariffs themselves because it leads to a pullback in economic activity.

One of the most frustrating things about trade wars is how they often fail to achieve their intended goals. Tariffs might protect a specific industry in the short term, but they do so at the expense of the broader economy. And in many cases, the industries being "protected" don't become more competitive. Instead, they rely on continued government intervention to stay afloat, creating a cycle of dependency that's hard to break.

What makes this even worse is the retaliatory nature of trade wars. When one country imposes tariffs, the other fires back with tariffs of its own. This tit-for-tat approach turns into a lose-lose situation. Businesses in both countries get caught in the crossfire, and consumers on both sides pay the price. It's a downward spiral that hurts everyone involved. Even the sectors that tariffs are supposed to help often find themselves struggling because they face reduced demand in retaliating markets.

Trade wars create a false sense of security for domestic industries while undermining the overall health of the economy. The costs are high, the benefits are limited, and the long-term consequences can be devastating. Businesses lose their competitive edge, consumers face higher prices, and economies get stuck in a cycle of retaliation and instability.

Retaliation Is A Losing Strategy

Retaliating in a trade war might feel like the natural thing to do. When another country imposes tariffs or trade barriers, the first instinct is to hit back with equal force. It feels like standing up for yourself, showing strength, and protecting your own industries. But in reality, retaliation in a trade war is more like throwing punches in a fight where everyone ends up bloodied. It might look tough in the moment, but it almost always leaves you worse off.

One of the biggest problems with retaliation is that it escalates the conflict. Trade wars are a cycle of action and reaction, and each round makes the situation more damaging. When one country imposes tariffs, the other responds in kind, leading to a tit-for-tat exchange that spirals out of control. This kind of escalation doesn't solve the original problem; it just amplifies it. The longer the trade war drags on, the more harm it does to both sides. Businesses are forced to deal with constant uncertainty, consumers face higher prices, and economic growth slows down.

Another issue is that retaliation often hurts your own people more than it hurts the other side. When you impose tariffs, you're effectively increasing the cost of goods for your own consumers and businesses. Take agriculture as an example. If Canada were to retaliate against US tariffs by imposing its own on American agricultural products, Canadian consumers would end up paying more for food. At the same time, Canadian farmers who rely on exporting their goods to the US could face new barriers, making it harder for them to compete. The very people you're trying to protect end up caught in the crossfire.

Retaliation also distracts from finding real solutions. Instead of addressing the underlying issues that make your economy vulnerable to trade disputes, you get caught up in a game of economic one-upmanship. This kind of reactive strategy doesn't build resilience or strength. It's a short-term fix that creates long-term problems. A more effective approach would be to focus on strengthening your own economy and protecting your people from the fallout, rather than trying to hurt the other side.

Retaliatory measures can also damage relationships with trade partners and allies. Trade wars don't happen in isolation. Other countries are watching, and your actions can influence how they perceive you as a partner. If Canada were to retaliate aggressively, it could strain relationships with other nations that might otherwise have been supportive. This could make it harder to negotiate future trade deals or build coalitions to address global trade issues.

Another important consideration is that retaliation often doesn't have the desired effect. The goal of imposing tariffs in response to a trade war is usually to pressure the other country into backing down. But that rarely happens. Instead, both sides dig in their heels, leading to a prolonged standoff. The other country might even double down on its own tariffs, making the situation worse. Meanwhile, the industries and consumers you're trying to protect continue to suffer.

Retaliation can give the appearance of doing something without actually solving anything. It's a performative move that plays well politically but doesn't address the root causes of the conflict. People might feel a sense of satisfaction seeing their government hit back, but that feeling fades quickly when the economic consequences start to pile up. A better approach is to stay focused on long-term strategies that build economic stability and protect the most vulnerable, rather than getting caught up in the back-and-forth of a trade war.

Retaliation isn't about winning; it's about reacting. And reacting isn't the same as leading. If Canada wants to navigate a trade war successfully, it needs to step back from the instinct to retaliate and focus on what really matters: protecting its people, strengthening its economy, and staying prepared for whatever comes next.

Avoid Escalation And Minimize Economic Harm

When faced with a trade war, the first instinct is often to strike back. But when you choose not to engage, you're actually protecting yourself from getting dragged deeper into the conflict. By avoiding retaliation, you prevent the situation from escalating into something more harmful. Trade wars tend to build on themselves. One tariff leads to another, and each measure adds more economic pain on both sides. When you don't engage, you stop that cycle before it takes hold. The economy is fragile, and every new round of tariffs and counter-tariffs compounds the damage. Not retaliating lets you avoid this spiral, giving your country a better chance to ride out the storm.

Another benefit of non-engagement is that it keeps the focus on protecting your own economy rather than getting involved in a damaging back-and-forth. If you don't retaliate, you're not putting your industries and consumers in a position where they have to deal with higher costs and uncertainty. Tariffs and trade barriers don't just hurt the target; they hurt the country imposing them too. When you stay out of the tit-for-tat game, you're sparing businesses and consumers from the burden of rising prices and disruptions in supply chains. That helps keep the economy steady, even in the face of pressure from abroad.

Choosing not to engage also preserves important trade relationships. In the middle of a trade war, it can be easy to think that hitting back is the only way to defend your interests. But this often leads to broken relationships with key partners. When you avoid engaging, you're keeping the door open for negotiations, future agreements, and long-term cooperation. Even if a country imposes tariffs, it doesn't mean you need to follow suit. By choosing a non-confrontational approach, you're showing that you're not looking for a fight. You're not closing off future opportunities by burning bridges.

Non-engagement also helps maintain stability within your own borders. Escalating a trade war can create widespread uncertainty. Businesses may hesitate to invest, hiring could slow down, and consumers might start to tighten their belts. When the economy slows down, it impacts everyone. By choosing not to retaliate, you minimize that uncertainty. You give businesses the breathing room to continue operating as usual and allow consumers to keep spending without worrying about the next round of price hikes. In times of uncertainty, stability is key. Non-engagement is one of the simplest ways to ensure your economy stays on track while others are fighting it out.

Choosing non-engagement also allows you to focus on strengthening your own economy in ways that don't involve fighting trade battles. Instead of retaliating, you can invest in policies that help people and businesses thrive, such as addressing the affordability crisis, improving social safety nets, and supporting innovation. By working on these things, you build a stronger economy that can weather external pressures, whether from a trade war or anything else. It's a proactive approach that focuses on long-term resilience rather than getting caught up in short-term skirmishes.

Sometimes, the best way to win isn't to fight at all. In a trade war, it's easy to think that retaliation is the answer, but in reality, non-engagement is a smarter strategy. It avoids the risks of escalation, shields the economy from unnecessary harm, and keeps the focus on building a stronger, more resilient nation. Rather than sinking into a conflict that only causes harm, Canada can stand back, stay steady, and focus on what really matters.

Corporate Interests And Trade War Vulnerability

Corporate interests have played a significant role in making Canada vulnerable to trade war tactics, whether they fully recognize it or not. Over the years, corporate interests have pushed for policies that keep wages low and avoid paying their fair share of taxes. In doing so, they have created an economic environment where the average Canadian worker is left unprepared to face the kind of pressures that come with a trade war. The Canadian worker should be seen as a strong ally in these economic challenges, but instead, they are often sidelined in favour of profit-driven decisions. When workers aren't paid fair wages and corporations aren't contributing their share to the public good, the entire country feels the ripple effects. This leaves Canada in a weakened position, making it harder for citizens to resist external economic pressures like those that would come in the form of tariffs and trade wars.

By choosing to cut corners on wages and avoid tax contributions, Canadian Industry has not just harmed the workers themselves but also made the country less resilient as a whole. When wages are stagnant or too low to keep up with rising costs, Canadians find themselves less able to weather economic storms. They are already living paycheck to paycheck, so when the costs of goods and services go up due to a trade war, they feel it even more acutely. Without enough financial cushion, it becomes difficult for workers to push back against economic pressures, leaving them exposed to the whims of international trade disputes. Instead of having a strong, empowered workforce capable of navigating tough times, the system has left them vulnerable, further weakening Canada's position in the global economy.

The disconnect between Canadian Industry and the average worker is a fundamental part of why Canada remains vulnerable to the forces of globalization. Until these two groups recognize that their fates are intertwined, Canada will continue to suffer. The workers in this country are the backbone of its economy, and yet, time and again, corporate interests prioritize short-term profits over long-term stability. This approach erodes the economic foundation of the nation, leaving workers without the resources they need to push back when faced with external threats. Without a fair exchange of wages and corporate responsibility, the country loses out on the economic strength that could help it weather external crises, like trade wars, and build a more stable, resilient economy.

It's not just about wages and taxes, though. It's about the overall attitude of Canadian Industry towards the Canadian workforce. If corporations continue to view workers as expendable parts of the machine, and if they continue to undercut those who create the value, there's no real incentive for the workers to stand strong when the pressure mounts. Instead, they may feel powerless or even resigned, unsure of how to navigate a world that feels stacked against them. But if Canadian Industry started to see the value in paying fair wages, investing in workers, and contributing to the country's prosperity through taxes, the whole economy would be better equipped to resist the kind of pressures that come with a trade war. A prosperous workforce means a stronger economy, which in turn means better resilience in the face of outside threats.

Canada's ongoing struggle with globalization has much to do with this fundamental disconnect between Canadian Industry and its workers. Globalization may seem like an inevitable force, but it doesn't have to destroy local economies. When workers are properly compensated and businesses contribute to the system that supports them, there's a much better chance of finding a balance where both sides benefit. But as long as Canadian Industry continues to undermine the economic security of its workers, Canada will always be on the back foot when it comes to handling external pressures like trade wars.

Without a shift towards collaboration, Canada will continue to suffer, and the workers who are the lifeblood of this country will be left in the lurch.

Building International Alliances

Canada has long been drawn into the economic conflicts of other nations, particularly in relation to the United States. The trade war with China is a perfect example. While the US frames these tensions as matters of national security, the reality is that they are more about maintaining US global economic dominance. Canada, by being pulled into this conflict, risks weakening its own economic standing. It's not just about security; it's about the United States' desire to maintain its position as the global economic leader. For Canada, aligning itself with the US in this way is more about supporting their interests than protecting its own. The real question for Canada is whether it wants to continue being dragged into these battles or whether it wants to break free and form its own path, one that benefits its citizens and its economy without getting caught in the geopolitical games of larger powers.

Building alliances with other nations who are also negatively affected by US trade policies could be a smart move for Canada. By recognizing that countries like China, and even others in Europe and elsewhere, are dealing with the same issues stemming from US tariffs and protectionist policies, Canada can step into a leadership role in fostering cooperation between nations that are also caught in the crossfire. These alliances don't just serve as a counterweight to US aggression but also provide a platform for creating new economic partnerships that are more balanced and mutually beneficial. Canada doesn't need to be part of the US-led economic battles to ensure its place in the global economy. Instead, by working with countries affected in similar ways, Canada could create its own network of trade partners who are less likely to use economic power as a weapon and more likely to prioritize fairness and stability.

The US, for all its power, is not the only game in town. By distancing itself from the conflict and seeking out partnerships with countries like China, Canada can safeguard its economic future. This doesn't mean abandoning its relationship with the US, but rather choosing to diversify its alliances. Canada's position in the global market doesn't have to be defined by the whims of US trade policy. By building alliances with nations that are similarly disadvantaged by US tariffs and trade restrictions, Canada can protect its own interests while also contributing to the creation of a more balanced, fair, and sustainable global trading system.

The real opportunity for Canada lies in its ability to chart its own course. As the US pushes forward with its own agenda, Canada should focus on creating a future where it doesn't rely so heavily on the US for its economic well-being. This means seeking out alternative trading partners, looking beyond the borders of its closest ally, and making it clear that it won't be dragged into every trade conflict the US decides to engage in. Canada's economic future should not be hostage to the political and economic strategies of another nation, especially when those strategies often prioritize the preservation of power rather than the long-term welfare of global citizens.

The key to Canada's success in this new global economy lies in its ability to form these alliances, protect its economic interests, and avoid unnecessary conflicts. By standing back from trade wars and refocusing on relationships that are more balanced and less driven by the pursuit of economic domination, Canada can build a more stable and sustainable economic future. The strength of its position won't come from fighting wars that don't serve its interests but from finding new ways to engage with the world on its own terms. In a world where the US is flexing its muscles in trade, Canada's best move is to step away from the battlefield and instead focus on creating lasting, meaningful partnerships that offer real economic security for its people.

Overview Of The Current Global Situation

The current global situation is one of significant tension, especially when it comes to trade. The United States, as the world's largest economy, has long used its economic power as a tool of influence, but over the past few years, the use of that power has intensified. The US has been increasingly involved in trade disputes with major economies, notably China, the European Union, and even its traditional allies like Canada. At the heart of these conflicts is the US's desire to preserve its economic dominance while reshaping global trade to its advantage. Canada, as a close neighbour and one of the US's largest trading partners, finds itself caught in the middle of these ongoing economic battles.

These trade disputes often revolve around tariffs, trade imbalances, intellectual property concerns, and other measures that the US has used to challenge what it perceives as unfair trading practices. For instance, the trade war between the US and China has escalated to the point where both countries have imposed tariffs on hundreds of billions of dollars worth of goods. This has disrupted global supply chains and forced other countries to choose sides or adapt to the changing landscape of international trade. Canada, being so intertwined with the US economically, has been directly impacted by these tensions.

The situation for Canada is complex. As a country that relies heavily on trade with the US, particularly in industries like manufacturing, agriculture, and natural resources, any disruption in the relationship with its southern neighbour is immediately felt. On top of that, Canada is part of a larger network of trade agreements, including the USMCA (formerly NAFTA), that ties it to the US but also opens the door for more negotiation and tension. As the US pushes its economic agenda, Canada must balance the need to maintain a good relationship with the US while also ensuring its own economic interests are protected.

What complicates matters further is the global shift in trade dynamics. While the US has sought to exert more control over global trade, countries like China, the EU, and others have been working to create their own alliances and trade networks that bypass US influence. Canada, despite being geographically close to the US, risks being left behind if it doesn't find ways to navigate this changing world order. The growing influence of China, for example, creates a dilemma for Canada as it seeks to balance its relationship with the US while also considering new opportunities in Asia.

This creates a precarious situation for Canada. The country finds itself in the middle of a trade war that is not of its making, yet it is forced to deal with the economic fallout. Canada is impacted by tariffs and other trade measures that the US imposes on other countries, as well as those the US imposes on Canada itself. In this environment, Canada must figure out how to maintain its economic health while navigating the complexities of international trade disputes, and doing so without engaging in retaliation or escalating tensions further. The challenge is not just about dealing with the fallout from a US trade war but also about ensuring that Canada doesn't become an easy target for economic pressures in the future.

Linking The COVID-19 Pandemic To Trade Wars

When we look back at the COVID-19 pandemic, one thing became clear: nations, even the wealthiest ones, are not immune to global disruptions. The pandemic forced countries to rethink how they protect their citizens and economies. Governments around the world had to come up with creative strategies to keep their economies afloat while simultaneously protecting the health and wellbeing of their people. This included lockdowns, stimulus packages, direct financial support to individuals, and reshoring supply chains. What became apparent was that when the world is shaken by a crisis, nations have the power and the responsibility to shield their citizens from its worst effects.

Fast forward to today, and we are facing a different kind of global disruption: trade wars. While not a pandemic in the traditional sense, trade wars have the same disruptive impact. Like a viral outbreak that spreads across borders, a trade war can cause ripple effects throughout the global economy, impacting businesses, workers, and entire nations. Tariffs, sanctions, and trade restrictions can have devastating effects on economies, creating uncertainty and rising costs for both consumers and businesses. But just as with the pandemic, nations can adopt strategies to protect their people and economies from these impacts.

During the pandemic, countries quickly realized they had to become more self-reliant. Governments around the world started to prioritize securing supplies of essential goods, like medical equipment and food. They took steps to ensure that their citizens had access to the basics even as the global supply chain was disrupted. In some cases, nations developed policies to reduce their dependence on foreign trade partners for critical products. Similarly, in the face of a trade war, Canada can look to strategies that foster self-sufficiency and reduce dependence on one dominant trading partner. The goal is to make sure that Canada has the resources it needs to weather the storm, without having to depend on the whims of foreign governments or unstable trade relationships.

The pandemic also highlighted the importance of having a resilient economy. Countries that had strong social safety nets and diversified industries were able to better handle the economic fallout. For Canada, the lesson is clear: we cannot afford to put all of our economic eggs in one basket. Diversifying trade relationships, supporting local industries, and strengthening the country's internal economy are all vital steps in preparing for future disruptions, whether they come in the form of pandemics or trade wars. A resilient economy means that when a crisis hits, whether it's a pandemic or a trade war, the country can better protect its citizens, minimize harm, and keep things running smoothly.

Nations have shown that they can take control in the face of global disruptions. The strategies they used during the pandemic prove that it's possible to adapt, protect citizens, and even emerge stronger. Trade wars, much like pandemics, are a form of disruption that countries need to be ready for. But just as the world's nations found ways to limit the damage of COVID-19, Canada can take steps to protect itself from the economic fallout of a trade war. It's all about strategic planning, diversifying resources, and being prepared to weather the storm without engaging in a destructive cycle of retaliation.

Lessons From The COVID-19 Pandemic

When we reflect on the COVID-19 pandemic, it's clear that the world faced an unprecedented challenge. Yet, amid the chaos, nations found ways to protect their citizens and their economies. Some of the strategies used during the pandemic were more effective than others, but there's no doubt that the experience offers valuable lessons that can be applied in different contexts, including in dealing with trade wars. For Canada, these lessons can help us develop a strong response to the economic challenges posed by a trade war with the US, ultimately positioning us to come out stronger.

One of the biggest takeaways from the pandemic was the importance of having a robust social safety net. Countries that had strong healthcare systems, unemployment benefits, and direct financial support were able to shield their citizens from the worst effects of the crisis. Canada has always had a relatively strong social safety net, but the pandemic underscored just how vital it is to have these protections in place when global shocks occur. In the event of a trade war, Canada could take a page from the pandemic playbook by ensuring that its citizens are financially supported. This might mean expanding social programs like unemployment insurance, providing direct cash assistance to those most affected, or offering support to businesses that are struggling to survive in a climate of uncertainty.

Another important lesson from the pandemic was the need for self-sufficiency, particularly when it comes to essential goods. At the start of the pandemic, we saw countries scrambling to secure supplies of medical equipment and personal protective gear. Nations that were able to quickly ramp up domestic production or diversify their sources of supply fared better than those that were overly dependent on global supply chains. Canada could apply this same strategy in a trade war. By investing in domestic industries and reducing our reliance on foreign goods, especially from the US, Canada would be better equipped to handle disruptions in the supply chain caused by tariffs or trade restrictions. This could involve expanding local manufacturing capabilities, supporting Canadian farmers and manufacturers, and ensuring that essential goods can be produced within our borders.

During the pandemic, we also saw countries like New Zealand and Taiwan take proactive measures to control the situation before it spiralled out of control. They acted quickly to put policies in place that minimized the spread of the virus and protected their economies from the worst impacts. Canada could learn from these nations in how to address a trade war. By taking preemptive steps to reduce the potential damage of a trade war, such as diversifying trade partnerships, negotiating favourable trade deals with other countries, and implementing economic policies that protect vulnerable sectors of the economy, Canada can position itself to withstand the pressure of a trade war without engaging in tit-for-tat retaliation.

One of the most effective strategies used by some countries during the pandemic was the clear and transparent communication between governments and their citizens. Nations like South Korea and Germany were able to keep their citizens informed and engaged in the process, which helped build public trust and cooperation. Canada could use this approach during a trade war by ensuring that citizens are kept in the loop about the situation, the measures being taken to protect them, and how they can help support the country's efforts. Clear communication helps to maintain stability and prevent panic, which is especially important in times of economic stress.

The pandemic also demonstrated the power of international cooperation. Countries that worked together to share resources, information, and expertise were able to respond more effectively. Canada, though geographically close to the US, could expand its relationships with other countries to mitigate the risks of a trade war. By strengthening ties with trading partners like the EU, Mexico, and emerging markets in Asia, Canada can diversify its economic relationships and reduce the risk of being overly reliant on one country. This approach not only helps Canada weather the storm but also opens up new opportunities for growth and development in global markets.

Canada's response to a trade war with the US doesn't have to be one of retaliation. By drawing on the lessons learned from the pandemic, we can create a more resilient, self-sufficient, and forward-thinking economy. With the right policies, support for our citizens, and proactive strategies, Canada can turn a trade war into an opportunity to strengthen its position on the global stage and emerge more powerful than ever.

Diversifying Trade Relationships

When the pandemic hit, countries like New Zealand quickly understood the importance of diversifying their supply chains and trade partners. They saw that relying too heavily on one source of goods, or one trading partner, made them vulnerable to disruptions. Canada, too, needs to take a similar approach when it comes to trade, especially considering the ongoing pressures we face from the US. The more Canada can create new trade alliances, the less vulnerable we become to the whims of any one country, even if that country happens to be our closest neighbour and largest trading partner.

Canada has traditionally leaned heavily on its relationship with the US, and for good reason. The proximity, shared interests, and established trade frameworks like NAFTA have made the US a cornerstone of our economic well-being. But when you put all your eggs in one basket, you run the risk of that basket being knocked over. We saw this with the pandemic, where countries that had diversified their supply chains found themselves in a better position to weather the storm. Similarly, when it comes to trade, Canada can no longer afford to put all of its economic eggs in the US basket. As tensions rise between the US and other countries, especially over trade, Canada needs to start building relationships with nations that are also facing pressure from the US.

The need for diversification is even more pressing when you look at the global landscape. While Canada is geographically close to the US, other countries in the world are facing similar economic and trade pressures. Countries in the European Union, Southeast Asia, and Latin America are also looking to lessen their reliance on the US. By partnering with these nations, Canada can build a network of trade relationships that strengthens our position on the global stage. For example, Canada already has strong trade agreements with the EU, like the Comprehensive Economic and Trade Agreement (CETA), but there is still untapped potential in that partnership. Strengthening these ties and exploring new trade opportunities with countries in Asia and Latin America would help Canada expand its economic footprint.

One way to approach this diversification is through creating new trade agreements that aren't just about raw materials or traditional sectors but focus on emerging industries, like technology, green energy, and advanced manufacturing. These industries are the future, and countries that can build strong connections in these areas will be better positioned to thrive in the coming decades. By proactively seeking out trade partnerships in these sectors, Canada can stay ahead of the curve and diversify its economy in a way that protects it from future economic shocks.

Another key benefit of diversifying trade relationships is that it makes Canada less susceptible to external pressures. When the US threatens tariffs or other trade measures, it's easy for Canada to feel cornered because of the sheer size and power of our neighbour. But if Canada has multiple strong trade relationships, we can better withstand those pressures. For instance, if the US tries to impose tariffs on Canadian products, Canada could look to its trade partners in the EU or Asia to pick up the slack and absorb some of the losses. In doing so, we not only protect our own economy but also send a clear message that Canada is not a country that can be bullied into submission.

Diversifying trade relationships also provides Canada with more leverage in negotiations. Right now, Canada's position in trade talks with the US is often weakened by our dependence on that single relationship. However, if Canada can present itself as part of a broader network of international trade partnerships, it will have more bargaining power. We could, for example, negotiate trade deals that benefit Canada as part of a larger trade block, ensuring that our interests are better represented and that we have alternatives if things go sour with the US.

Diversification is not just about avoiding risk; it's about actively creating opportunities for growth and development. The pandemic showed the importance of adaptability, and the same principle applies to trade. By building new partnerships with countries facing similar challenges, Canada can protect itself from the volatility of the global economy and position itself for future success. We need to move away from the mindset of relying on one country and start thinking more globally, expanding our relationships and looking for new avenues of trade that will benefit all Canadians.

Domestic Economic Support

When a trade war heats up, it's easy to think about the immediate costs to industries and workers who get caught in the crossfire. Canada would be no different if a full-blown trade war with the US breaks out. But instead of simply reacting and engaging in a retaliatory battle, there's an opportunity for Canada to put strategies in place that could actually shield our domestic industries and workers from the worst effects of this economic disruption. One way to do this is by using targeted economic measures similar to what we saw during the pandemic, such as subsidies for key sectors, tax breaks for small businesses, or direct financial assistance for industries that need it most. These measures can keep Canadian businesses afloat while they ride out the storm.

The pandemic showed us how government intervention can make a huge difference when economies face unexpected shocks. The stimulus packages that were rolled out across the world, including Canada, helped keep businesses alive and workers employed even when it seemed like things were spiralling out of control. This kind of intervention can also work when it comes to trade wars. If Canada faces tariffs or other trade disruptions that hurt local industries, targeted support can help protect those industries and maintain jobs. Industries like agriculture, manufacturing, and tech might face different kinds of challenges, but targeted support, whether in the form of financial aid, tax relief, or other incentives, can help those businesses stay competitive even when external pressures are pushing hard against them.

One area where Canada could get creative is by providing subsidies to sectors most vulnerable to the impact of trade disruptions. For example, the agriculture sector often faces tariff increases when trade wars break out. By providing subsidies to farmers or food producers, Canada could help them lower their costs and stay competitive in both domestic and international markets. This kind of support would make it easier for Canadian producers to continue producing at a lower cost, keeping prices down for consumers while maintaining a strong, competitive edge against foreign competitors. It's a way to make sure our essential industries aren't decimated by policies that are beyond their control.

Tax breaks for small businesses could also play a big role in keeping Canada's domestic economy resilient during a trade war. Small businesses are often the hardest hit during times of economic uncertainty. While large corporations have the resources to absorb the blow or shift operations elsewhere, small businesses may not have that luxury. Tax breaks or direct financial support can help them survive the lean times, keep their employees on payroll, and avoid closures. Canada's small businesses are a backbone of the economy, and making sure they have the support they need could go a long way in maintaining the overall health of the economy.

There's also room for innovation when it comes to how Canada might protect key industries in the face of trade disruptions. The pandemic showed that when traditional markets dry up, countries can pivot to other sources of growth. The same approach can be applied in a trade war scenario. By investing in new sectors, like renewable energy, technology, or green industries, Canada can help its economy shift towards sectors that are less vulnerable to trade pressures. With the right investment in these growing fields, Canada can give industries the tools they need to thrive, even as traditional markets like the US become less predictable.

Government support is also crucial in protecting Canadian workers during a trade war. In the event of job losses or industry downturns, unemployment benefits, retraining programs, and relocation assistance can help workers adjust and stay afloat. This approach would focus on minimizing the negative impacts on everyday Canadians, ensuring they don't bear the brunt of the economic consequences. Ensuring a fair social safety net and support for retraining allows workers to remain part of the economy even if their previous industry takes a hit.

Targeted economic measures don't just keep businesses afloat; they can also help Canadian industries become more competitive in the long run. By investing in innovation, diversifying industries, and supporting workers and businesses, Canada can emerge stronger from a trade war. Rather than being swept up in the turmoil of global economic battles, Canada can focus on reinforcing its domestic economy and creating a sustainable future.

Strengthening Local Industries

When we look back at how the world responded to the pandemic, one of the key takeaways is the importance of local production. Countries were forced to deal with shortages of everything from medical supplies to food, and it quickly became clear how vulnerable global supply chains were. The pandemic really laid bare just how much we rely on foreign countries, and specifically the US, for essential goods and services. It wasn't just about being unprepared for a pandemic, it was about being overly dependent on outside sources for things that could, and should, be produced at home. Canada, like many other nations, had to scramble to secure the things we needed. In the face of a trade war, Canada finds itself in a similar situation. A strong focus on strengthening local industries and reducing dependence on the US and vulnerable global supply chains could make a huge difference in our resilience during economic disruptions.

Strengthening local industries isn't just a matter of creating jobs or boosting the economy, though those things are important. It's about giving ourselves the capacity to withstand external shocks, whether those come in the form of a trade war or another global crisis. If Canada's domestic industries can produce more of the goods and services we rely on, we won't be as at the mercy of the whims of other countries. This would mean a shift towards boosting production here at home, in sectors like agriculture, manufacturing, technology, and energy. By strengthening these industries, Canada would create more economic security for its people and businesses.

Take agriculture, for example. Canada is known for its vast expanses of farmland, but much of the food that Canadians consume is still imported. During the pandemic, this became an issue when supply chains were disrupted and we saw shortages of certain foods. By investing in local food production and building stronger infrastructure around it, Canada could reduce its reliance on food imports and create a more resilient food system. This doesn't mean Canada should stop trading internationally, but it does mean that Canada should focus on producing more of what it consumes. If we invest in local farmers, offer them the support they need, and reduce the red tape that hinders their growth, we can make sure the country is better equipped to handle trade disruptions, without leaving people scrambling to find food on the shelves.

Manufacturing is another key area where Canada could focus on becoming more self-sufficient. Over the years, Canada has outsourced much of its manufacturing to other countries, often to places where labour is cheaper. This has worked out in many ways, but when things go wrong, like during a trade war or a global crisis, it becomes clear how fragile these supply chains can be. Canada should take steps to bring more manufacturing back home, not necessarily to replace all of what we import but to build a stronger domestic base. This could mean investing in technologies that make manufacturing more efficient, providing incentives for businesses to move production back to Canada, and developing skilled labour forces to meet the needs of new industries. Strong domestic manufacturing would mean that Canada is not so dependent on other countries for things like electronics, machinery, and medical supplies, which are essential for the functioning of the economy, especially in times of crisis.

Tech is another sector where local production could be a game-changer. The digital world is growing faster than ever, and Canada has the potential to be a major player in this space. But like many other industries, Canada often relies on the US for access to key technologies and services. By strengthening local tech industries, through support for startups, investment in research and development, and creating a favourable environment for tech innovation, Canada could reduce its dependency on foreign tech companies. This would not only bolster the economy but also ensure that Canada remains competitive in an increasingly globalized world, especially in areas like artificial intelligence, cybersecurity, and clean tech, which are likely to be vital for the future.

Energy is another critical area where strengthening local industries could provide Canada with much-needed resilience. Canada is rich in natural resources, yet we still rely on imported energy, particularly oil and gas. If Canada can increase its own energy production, especially through renewable sources like wind and solar, it could not only reduce reliance on foreign energy imports but also strengthen its position in a trade war. We could build a more sustainable and secure energy future that reduces the vulnerability to global energy market fluctuations and helps the environment at the same time. By bolstering industries in clean energy, Canada would not just protect its citizens from the impact of trade wars, but also position itself as a leader in a growing global sector.

Ultimately, the more Canada can produce domestically, the less it will have to rely on the US and other countries for essential goods and services. By strengthening local industries in key sectors, Canada can create a more self-sufficient economy that is more resilient in the face of global disruptions, whether that be a trade war, a pandemic, or another crisis. It's not about cutting off trade with other nations but rather about finding a balance where Canada is strong enough to withstand external pressures and maintain its economic sovereignty. This kind of investment in local industries will take time, but it's a strategy that pays off in the long run and ensures that Canada is not caught off guard when the next global disruption comes around.

Investing In Innovation And Technology

During the pandemic, many countries accelerated their technological developments and pushed for digitization in ways that were previously unthinkable. It wasn't just about making life easier during a time of crisis; it was about making sure that they could survive the economic disruptions that came with it. Technology became the lifeline for businesses, governments, and individuals alike, and it showed just how crucial innovation is to resilience in times of global upheaval. For Canada, this is a lesson that we should take seriously, especially as we consider how to navigate the challenges of a trade war with the US. Investing in innovation and technology could be the key to ensuring long-term economic resilience. If we focus on growing our own technological and manufacturing sectors, Canada would be better equipped to weather future disruptions, whether they come in the form of trade wars or global crises.

Looking at how other countries responded to the pandemic gives us a clear picture of the path forward. Nations that were able to adapt quickly were the ones that had already laid the groundwork in digital infrastructure and technological innovation. These countries didn't just react to the crisis; they had invested in innovation long before the pandemic hit. Canada could learn from that. By prioritizing investment in our technological and manufacturing sectors now, we could foster long-term economic resilience and position ourselves as leaders in emerging industries. This would not only help us become more self-sufficient but also reduce our reliance on global supply chains, which have proven to be fragile during times of crisis.

Investing in innovation doesn't just mean pouring money into big tech companies or startups; it's about creating an ecosystem where innovation can thrive at every level. Canada has the potential to be a hub for technological advancements, but we need to make it easier for entrepreneurs and businesses to succeed. This could mean providing incentives for businesses to invest in research and development, ensuring that our universities and research institutions are equipped to push the boundaries of what's possible, and fostering a culture that encourages risk-taking and experimentation. The more we can support innovation within our borders, the more likely we are to build industries that can compete on the global stage and reduce our dependency on countries like the US.

Manufacturing also has a huge role to play in this equation. The pandemic exposed the vulnerability of global supply chains, and Canada was no exception. We rely heavily on imports for everything from electronics to medical supplies, and this leaves us exposed to the whims of other countries, especially when trade tensions rise. By investing in manufacturing technology, Canada can reduce its reliance on foreign-made goods and increase our own production capabilities. This doesn't mean we should abandon international trade altogether; it means we should be smart about where we put our efforts. Canada has the ability to develop high-tech manufacturing capabilities that can produce advanced products right here at home. With the right investments in automation, robotics, and AI-driven production methods, Canada can not only become more self-sufficient but also more competitive on the global market.

This kind of investment will also create jobs and stimulate the economy in ways that can provide long-term benefits. Technological advancements are driving forces behind the creation of new industries, and Canada can be at the forefront of these developments. Clean energy, artificial intelligence, advanced manufacturing, and biotechnology are just a few of the fields where Canada has the potential to lead. By investing in these areas, Canada could become a global powerhouse in industries that are only going to grow in importance. This is especially true when we look at the rapid rise of green technologies and sustainable industries. If Canada can lead in these fields, it won't just protect us from trade disruptions; it will create new opportunities and jobs for Canadians in the process.

Focusing on technology and innovation also means investing in the workforce. As industries evolve, the skills needed to thrive in them will change too. This is an opportunity for Canada to ensure that its citizens have access to the training and education needed to succeed in a high-tech world. By making sure that workers have the skills necessary for the industries of tomorrow, we can help bridge the gap between today's economy and the economy of the future. This also means investing in small businesses and entrepreneurs who are often the ones driving innovation from the ground up. By creating an environment where startups can flourish, Canada will encourage the kinds of breakthroughs that lead to economic resilience.

In the face of a trade war or any other kind of economic disruption, Canada's ability to adapt will depend heavily on our technological and industrial capabilities. If we invest in these sectors now, we can ensure that we're not left behind when global events start to unfold. Canada doesn't have to be a bystander in the global economy; it has the potential to be a leader. By embracing innovation and technology, we can create a more resilient economy that is better equipped to handle the challenges of the future. The key is to start investing today and make sure that we're not just reacting to the world as it changes but actively shaping the future we want to see.

Self-Sufficiency In Key Industries

The pandemic was a wake-up call for a lot of countries, including Canada. When borders closed and global supply chains were disrupted, it became clear how vulnerable we were when it came to certain key industries. In moments like these, we realized how reliant we had become on other nations for essentials like medical supplies, food, and even basic technology. It shouldn't have taken a global health crisis to highlight these vulnerabilities, but now that it has, it's a chance for Canada to rethink how we approach our own self-sufficiency. We need to prioritize strengthening the critical sectors that could protect us during times of economic strain, sectors like healthcare, food production, and technology. If we can focus on becoming more self-sufficient in these areas, we'll be much better positioned to handle not just global pandemics but also the economic fallout of something like a trade war.

First, let's look at healthcare. The pandemic exposed just how much Canada depends on other countries for medical supplies, from simple items like masks and gloves to more complex ones like ventilators and vaccines. We saw firsthand how quickly the supply chain can break down when countries scramble to secure resources for their own populations. For Canada, this means that we need to start investing in domestic production of healthcare essentials. We have the capacity to manufacture these items right here, so there's no reason why we should rely on other countries. By prioritizing self-sufficiency in healthcare, we could avoid the kind of shortages we saw during the pandemic and be much better prepared for future emergencies, whether they're health-related or driven by trade tensions. A robust domestic healthcare industry would also give us more control over our own medical supply chains, which is important for both security and stability.

Then there's food production. Canada is blessed with vast amounts of arable land, and we're one of the world's largest agricultural producers. Despite this, a lot of our food supply is tied to imports from other countries. During the pandemic, we saw how disruptions in global food supply chains affected grocery store shelves and prices. If a trade war with the US escalates, Canada could be at the mercy of export restrictions or rising tariffs that would make food even more expensive and less available. This makes it essential for Canada to look inward and boost our own food production. Strengthening domestic agriculture and food processing could help ensure that Canadians have access to affordable, high-quality food, even if global trade becomes strained. It's not just about growing more food; it's about having the infrastructure and capacity to process and distribute it efficiently within our borders. That way, we're not relying on imports to feed our population, and we're better insulated from the economic effects of a trade war.

Another area where self-sufficiency is crucial is technology. As technology plays an increasingly larger role in our daily lives, it's important that Canada is able to develop and manufacture its own tech products rather than relying on other countries. The pandemic pushed many businesses and services into the digital realm, highlighting just how much we depend on technology for everything from work to healthcare. Yet, much of the technology we rely on comes from outside our borders, particularly from the US, China, and other tech giants. In the event of a trade war, Canada could find itself facing significant disruptions in the availability of technology products and services. This is why it's so important for Canada to start fostering its own tech industry. This could mean investing in research and development, supporting Canadian startups, and ensuring that we have the necessary infrastructure in place to produce high-tech goods domestically. By developing our own technological capacity, we can reduce our dependence on foreign tech and avoid potential disruptions caused by trade tensions.

Focusing on self-sufficiency in these key sectors, healthcare, food production, and technology, would make Canada much more resilient to global disruptions, whether they're caused by a pandemic or a trade war. A lot of the lessons from the pandemic are still fresh in our minds, and now is the time to act on them. We shouldn't wait for the next crisis to remind us of the importance of self-sufficiency. By taking steps now to strengthen these industries, Canada can protect its economy, its citizens, and its future. It's about making sure that we don't rely on others to meet our basic needs. Canada has the resources and the talent to become more self-sufficient, and it's in our best interest to do so. By focusing on these critical sectors, we can build an economy that is more resilient and better able to weather the economic impacts of any global disruption, including a trade war.

Strengthening The Social Safety Net

The social safety net is one of those things we often take for granted until we really need it. When something like a trade war hits, or even a global pandemic, it becomes clear just how important it is to have a system in place that supports people when things go wrong. For Canada, this means looking at how we can strengthen our social contract with citizens, ensuring that when crises occur, be it economic or otherwise, everyone is taken care of. If we're going to weather the storm of a trade war, we need to ensure that people aren't left behind and that the most vulnerable don't fall through the cracks. We need a safety net that's not just there to catch people when they're struggling, but also one that's proactive in preventing hardships from escalating.

One way to do this is by looking at something like guaranteed minimum income (GMI). GMI is an idea that's been gaining traction over the past few years, and for good reason. In the context of a trade war, where job losses and wage cuts are likely to become more common, GMI could provide Canadians with a financial cushion that helps them weather the economic fallout. It's not just about giving people money; it's about ensuring that no one is left struggling to make ends meet when their livelihood is threatened. GMI has the potential to level the playing field, providing a basic income to everyone, regardless of their circumstances. In doing so, it can help reduce poverty, encourage entrepreneurship, and even create a healthier, more productive society. When people know they have a financial safety net, they can take risks, pursue education, or even start their own businesses without the constant worry of where their next paycheck is coming from.

Beyond that, Canada can expand its healthcare and housing protections. The pandemic showed us just how important access to affordable healthcare is, especially during times of crisis. The last thing people should have to worry about when they're facing economic instability is whether or not they can afford to see a doctor or get the medication they need. Strengthening healthcare protections would mean ensuring that everyone has access to the care they need, regardless of their income or employment status. This goes hand-in-hand with making sure that housing is affordable and secure. Housing is another basic need that shouldn't be up for debate, especially in times of economic hardship. With a trade war potentially pushing more people into financial insecurity, it's crucial that the government works to ensure that housing remains accessible. Whether it's through rent control, subsidies for low-income families, or expanded affordable housing programs, making sure that people have a safe and stable place to live is one of the most fundamental ways the government can support its citizens.

The social safety net should also extend to people who are struggling to find work due to economic disruptions. This could mean strengthening unemployment insurance programs, providing retraining opportunities for workers displaced by changes in the economy, and creating pathways for people to transition into new industries. The government can help people adapt to changing circumstances by offering support for job seekers, from career counselling to funding for educational programs that equip people with the skills they need for the jobs of tomorrow. This is where investing in retraining programs and skills development is key. By supporting people in their efforts to find meaningful work, the government can help build a more resilient workforce, one that's prepared for whatever challenges the future may bring.

When we think about strengthening the social safety net, we're talking about more than just handing out aid when people fall on hard times. It's about creating a system that values the well-being of every Canadian, regardless of what the economy looks like or where global trade relationships stand. It's about building a stronger social contract between the government and the people, where everyone knows that the government has their back when the going gets tough. If we can create a more robust social safety net, we can help ensure that even when external forces like trade wars disrupt the economy, Canadians will be able to weather those disruptions without facing the worst outcomes. A well-supported population is a resilient one, and by strengthening our social contract, we can build a society that's more united and better prepared to face any challenge.

Canada's Strategic Role In Global Partnerships

Canada has always been in a unique position on the world stage, often seen as a middle power, neither a global superpower nor a small, isolated nation. This gives Canada the flexibility to forge relationships with a wide range of countries and act as a bridge between larger powers. In the context of a trade war, especially one with the United States, Canada's middle power status can be leveraged to build stronger relationships with other nations that find themselves similarly caught in the crossfire of US trade policies. Countries like China, the European Union, and emerging markets are already feeling the strain of shifting global trade dynamics. Canada, with its stable political environment, strong rule of law, and reputation for diplomacy, is in a prime position to foster relationships with these nations and build coalitions that benefit all parties involved.

For instance, Canada can build a stronger partnership with China. Despite the tensions between China and the US, both countries are integral to the global economy, and Canada could play a role in facilitating more economic cooperation between the two. By positioning itself as a neutral party, Canada could encourage dialogue and trade agreements that might not be possible if countries are locked in a direct dispute. Additionally, by engaging with China, Canada could tap into the growing Chinese market, which has long been a strategic goal. China's vast consumer base, expanding technological sector, and investment potential could be vital for Canada's economic diversification, particularly if trade with the US becomes increasingly unstable.

Similarly, Canada has the opportunity to strengthen its ties with the European Union, a bloc of nations that share similar democratic values and often align on international policies. With the US turning its focus inward under its trade policies, Canada could make a concerted effort to build deeper economic, political, and cultural relationships with the EU. Whether through trade agreements, joint ventures in technology and innovation, or shared goals around climate change, Canada and the EU have a lot to offer each other. The EU, for its part, has been trying to balance its economic relationship with the US, so Canada could act as an intermediary, working to align the interests of both sides while also finding ways to stand up to US protectionism in a way that doesn't harm the economies of smaller nations.

Emerging markets, too, present an opportunity for Canada to diversify its trade and foster relationships beyond the US. Nations in Africa, Latin America, and parts of Asia are growing rapidly and becoming more economically significant. Canada, with its wealth of natural resources, advanced technology, and education systems, can position itself as a partner for these nations. These emerging markets are particularly vulnerable to US trade policies that often involve tariffs and sanctions, which could hurt their ability to grow and develop. By fostering strong economic ties with these countries, Canada can create alternative markets for its goods and services, reducing reliance on the US and strengthening its global position.

Canada's role as a middle power is especially valuable in this context because it allows the country to act as a diplomatic conduit between larger powers, facilitating dialogue where others might fail. Canada can act as a voice for smaller nations in the international arena, advocating for fairer trade policies and working towards a more balanced global economy. Through multilateral forums like the United Nations, the G7, and the World Trade Organization, Canada can help shape the conversation around global trade, pushing for systems that benefit all nations and are not dictated by the economic whims of one superpower.

Ultimately, Canada's position as a middle power gives it the ability to influence global trade relations in a way that a larger power like the US cannot. By building and strengthening partnerships with countries that are also affected by US trade policies, Canada can reduce its own vulnerability to economic fallout from trade wars while contributing to the stability of the global economy. These partnerships can open up new trade opportunities, promote innovation, and ensure that Canada's interests are not tied solely to the whims of a single, increasingly unpredictable superpower. By acting as a diplomatic bridge between nations, Canada can help ensure that it remains a strong player on the world stage, even in the face of global trade disruption.

Building A Stronger, More Diverse Economy

The aftermath of a trade war, particularly one with the United States, could present Canada with a unique opportunity to reshape its economy and build a stronger, more resilient future. While it's easy to get caught up in the immediate pressures of such a conflict, the long-term strategy lies in what Canada does after the dust settles. Just as countries around the world found new paths forward after the pandemic disrupted global economies, Canada too can emerge from a trade war stronger, provided it makes the right moves to diversify and bolster its economic foundation. This isn't about getting dragged into the conflict itself, but about taking advantage of the shifting global landscape to foster a more sustainable and varied economy.

During the pandemic, many countries faced immense disruption, yet they adapted by focusing on economic diversification. For Canada, this means reducing its over-reliance on any single market or sector, particularly the US. One of the most important lessons from the pandemic is how vulnerable global supply chains are when they're overly concentrated in one region. Canada, with its vast resources and skilled labour force, can begin by investing in new sectors that are less susceptible to the whims of global trade conflicts. Renewable energy, green technologies, and advanced manufacturing are just a few examples of areas that could see significant growth if given the right support. Canada can focus on building sectors that provide jobs, stimulate innovation, and reduce the country's dependency on industries vulnerable to outside pressures.

Diversifying trade partnerships should be at the core of this strategy. By expanding beyond the US and building stronger relationships with emerging markets and other developed nations, Canada can create a network of economic ties that offers more stability and security. The pandemic highlighted the importance of having a diverse set of global partners. If one region is affected, there are others to turn to. Canada can invest in building stronger trade relationships with countries in Asia, Europe, and Africa, which would not only provide new markets for Canadian goods but also help reduce the risks associated with relying too heavily on one economic superpower.

Fostering innovation is another key strategy. Just as nations ramped up their technological advancements and digitization during the pandemic, Canada has the opportunity to invest in its own technological sector, particularly in fields like artificial intelligence, biotech, and clean tech. Investing in these areas would not only help diversify the economy but also position Canada as a leader in the global marketplace. Technology has the potential to make industries more efficient, create new job opportunities, and connect Canada with the rest of the world in new ways.

Moreover, strengthening local industries is a critical piece of the puzzle. During the pandemic, countries learned the importance of local production and self-sufficiency. By encouraging the growth of domestic industries, particularly in key sectors like healthcare, food production, and manufacturing, Canada can reduce its vulnerability to external shocks. This doesn't mean closing off from global trade entirely but ensuring that Canada has the capacity to meet its own needs in critical areas. By focusing on local production, Canada can enhance its resilience, providing more stability for its economy during future crises, whether economic or health-related.

Lastly, Canada's economic recovery and resilience will depend on its ability to invest in human capital. During the pandemic, countries that prioritized education and skills development were better equipped to face the challenges of a changing global economy. Canada needs to invest in its workforce, ensuring that workers are prepared for the future of work. This means not just retraining workers displaced by changes in trade but also ensuring that the next generation is equipped with the skills needed for emerging industries. Fostering innovation, supporting tech-focused startups, and investing in education and workforce development are essential for ensuring that Canada can weather any future storm, including the impacts of a trade war.

Canada's path forward after a trade war lies in its ability to harness the lessons learned from the global pandemic. The world has changed, and Canada has the chance to change with it, building a more diversified, resilient economy. By focusing on reducing reliance on any single market, investing in innovation, fostering local production, and prioritizing education and workforce development, Canada can emerge stronger and more secure, less susceptible to the shocks of global economic disruption. The challenge will be in how Canada chooses to respond, using this time not as an obstacle but as an opportunity to build something far more robust for the future.

Environmental And Social Sustainability

Canada has an opportunity to emerge stronger from a trade war not just by focusing on economic resilience but also by committing to environmental sustainability and social equity. This is about thinking long-term and recognizing that a country's true strength lies in how well it takes care of its people and its land. During the pandemic, many countries began to realize the importance of public welfare and sustainability. People were more aware than ever of the need for a robust healthcare system, safe working conditions, and a healthy environment. These lessons shouldn't be lost in the aftermath of a trade war; instead, they should be integrated into Canada's recovery strategy.

By prioritizing environmental sustainability, Canada can lead the way in creating a more green economy. The pandemic showed us that the planet is fragile and that our current way of doing business is not sustainable in the long run. The trade war may create economic pressures, but it can also serve as a catalyst for Canada to adopt more sustainable practices across all sectors. Imagine an economy that is not just focused on short-term gains but one that looks at long-term solutions for the environment. This could mean greater investment in clean energy, reducing carbon emissions, and transitioning to a circular economy that minimizes waste. By creating industries around renewable energy, electric vehicles, and sustainable agriculture, Canada can position itself as a leader in the global green economy, which could ultimately make it more competitive and less dependent on the volatile global market.

At the same time, social equity must play a central role in any economic recovery plan. The pandemic brought to light the stark inequalities in society. We saw how vulnerable populations were disproportionately affected by the virus, and those lessons shouldn't be forgotten. Canada has an opportunity to address these inequities head-on, ensuring that economic growth is inclusive and benefits all people, not just the wealthy or those in power. This could mean making healthcare more accessible, investing in affordable housing, and raising the minimum wage to ensure that no one is left behind. It's about creating a society where everyone has a fair shot at success, where people are not just surviving but thriving. A strong, equitable society is one where people feel secure and valued, and that in turn creates a stable environment for economic growth.

Incorporating environmental and social sustainability into the response to a trade war can help Canada become more self-sufficient and less vulnerable to outside pressures. When a country commits to these values, it reduces its dependence on foreign markets and becomes more resilient to global disruptions. Sustainable practices can create jobs and industries that are not just environmentally friendly but also socially responsible. Workers in these sectors can benefit from better wages, benefits, and working conditions, helping to close the wealth gap and create a more balanced economy. At the same time, the shift towards green industries can lead to technological innovation that strengthens Canada's position in global markets.

The key here is to recognize that the trade war is not just an economic challenge but a chance for Canada to rethink its entire approach to growth. This is a moment to focus on building a better, more sustainable future, not just recovering what was lost. By committing to environmental sustainability and social equity, Canada can create an economy that works for everyone and the planet, not just the few. The pandemic has taught us that real security comes from strong public welfare systems and sustainable practices. If Canada can build on these lessons and integrate them into its response to a trade war, it won't just survive; it will thrive.

A Re-Imagined Global Role For Canada

Canada has the potential to redefine its role on the global stage, one that is independent, influential, and based on principles of cooperation and mutual respect. For too long, Canada has found itself pulled into the orbit of US interests, often sidelining its own national priorities in the process. This has especially been evident in trade conflicts and international tensions where Canada's involvement has been shaped more by the demands of its southern neighbour than by its own strategic interests. But as global dynamics shift, there is a real opportunity for Canada to step back, reassess its position, and chart a new course that puts its own values and interests at the forefront.

Instead of being continually drawn into disputes that don't serve its long-term goals, Canada can play a more proactive role in fostering international cooperation. In a world increasingly divided by power struggles, Canada has the chance to be a bridge between nations, facilitating dialogue and collaboration. Its reputation for peacekeeping, diplomacy, and human rights gives it an edge when it comes to engaging with both established powers and emerging markets. Rather than aligning itself blindly with the US or any other dominant power, Canada could become a champion for multilateralism, pushing for solutions that benefit everyone, not just the few.

This shift would require a reevaluation of Canada's foreign policy, focusing on a more balanced approach that considers its own economic and political interests as much as it does the interests of others. Canada's wealth of natural resources, its commitment to sustainability, and its growing technological and innovation sectors position it well to take on a leadership role in the global economy. The world is looking for nations that can offer stability and cooperation in the face of rising tensions. Canada can position itself as a key player by leading on issues such as climate change, fair trade practices, and international peace efforts. By doing so, Canada can leverage its existing strengths and build new partnerships that allow it to flourish independently, while remaining a respected global partner.

Canada's relationship with the US will always be important, but it shouldn't define the country's entire foreign policy. The trade wars and international conflicts driven by US interests often put Canada in a compromising position, forcing it to make choices that aren't always in line with its own values or best interests. Moving forward, Canada has the chance to step away from this pattern and chart a path that reflects its own needs and aspirations. By focusing on partnerships that are mutually beneficial and by standing firm on issues like human rights, environmental sustainability, and fair trade, Canada can carve out a unique role for itself on the world stage.

Canada doesn't need to be a follower in global affairs. It has the tools and values to lead, and by focusing on cooperation and respect for all nations, it can foster relationships that are more meaningful and long-lasting. This approach won't just make Canada more independent but will also allow it to contribute to global stability in a way that aligns with its ideals. Through a re-imagined global role, Canada can not only survive a trade war but emerge stronger, more influential, and respected by the international community.

Socially Responsible Corporate Behaviour

Socially responsible corporate behaviour refers to the idea that companies should not only focus on making profits but also consider the impact their actions have on society, the environment, and the well-being of their workers. It's about businesses taking responsibility for how their operations affect the world around them and striving to make positive contributions, whether that's through sustainable practices, fair labour conditions, or supporting community initiatives. In today's global economy, this concept is more important than ever. As markets become more interconnected and the consequences of corporate actions ripple across borders, the public, governments, and consumers are increasingly holding companies accountable for their choices. There's a growing recognition that business success shouldn't come at the expense of people or the planet, and that businesses have a role to play in addressing the big challenges we face, from climate change to inequality.

But for socially responsible behaviour to truly take root across industries, regulation plays a vital role. Without some level of oversight, many companies might prioritize short-term profits over the long-term good. When profit is the only driver, it can be easy for businesses to cut corners in areas like environmental sustainability or worker compensation to save money. That's where regulation comes in. Government policies and laws set the framework within which businesses operate, ensuring that they meet certain standards that protect society and the environment. This isn't about stifling business growth or innovation. It's about guiding companies toward practices that benefit everyone, including their own long-term success. Regulations can make sure that fair wages are paid, that environmental standards are upheld, and that labour conditions are safe and humane. Without these regulations, businesses might ignore these important issues because they're not directly tied to their bottom line.

When businesses are left completely unregulated, they don't just have the potential to harm workers, communities, and the environment; they also end up hurting themselves in the process. In a fiercely competitive marketplace, companies often feel the pressure to outdo each other, sometimes at the expense of ethical practices. This can lead to a dangerous race to the bottom, where businesses slash costs by cutting corners, lowering wages, or ignoring environmental standards in order to undercut their competition. This behaviour can quickly become unsustainable, as companies that engage in such practices might see short-term profits, but at the cost of long-term stability. When the market is flooded with businesses that are cannibalizing each other in this way, it creates an unstable environment for everyone. Companies that follow ethical practices may find themselves out-priced or outperformed by those willing to exploit workers and the environment, and as a result, the entire industry becomes less sustainable, less resilient, and more prone to volatility.

This kind of unregulated competition can have real negative consequences for Canadians. It not only undermines the stability of Canadian industries but also makes the workforce more vulnerable. Lower wages, unsafe working conditions, and environmental degradation ultimately harm Canadian communities and taxpayers, leading to higher costs in the long run. When businesses disregard their social responsibilities, they often shift the burden onto the government and the public. Whether it's through the increased need for social services, the costs of cleaning up environmental damage, or the strain on the healthcare system due to poor working conditions, the public ends up paying for what should have been a business responsibility. By regulating businesses and enforcing socially responsible behaviour, we can ensure that industries aren't undermining each other in a race to the bottom, but instead, they are operating within a framework that promotes long-term stability, fair competition, and a healthier economy for all Canadians.

Widespread Benefits For All Canadians

When businesses in Canada commit to being socially responsible, it creates a ripple effect that benefits everyone. Paying fair wages and contributing their fair share of taxes is not just about doing what's right; it's about ensuring the overall health and prosperity of the country. For one, when workers are paid well, they have the means to invest in their own health, education, and wellbeing. A healthier, more educated workforce is naturally more productive. Workers with access to proper healthcare, education, and opportunities for growth are more likely to contribute meaningfully to the workplace, resulting in a stronger economy and more robust industries. They are able to innovate, think critically, and adapt to new challenges, qualities that are essential in a rapidly changing global landscape.

A corporate sector that embraces this kind of responsibility isn't just doing good for the people; it's doing good for itself. By ensuring that employees have what they need to thrive, companies create a more loyal and engaged workforce. When workers feel valued and see their employers taking part in making their communities better, it leads to higher morale, lower turnover, and better retention rates. This isn't just about making people feel good; it's about creating an environment where workers feel motivated to work harder and smarter. The positive culture that comes from fair wages and taxes creates a more stable, reliable workforce that companies can rely on for the long haul.

This kind of corporate responsibility also strengthens the country's resilience against outside pressures. Whether it's an economic crisis, a global pandemic, or a trade war, businesses that are socially responsible have a better chance of weathering the storm. They are more likely to have strong relationships with their employees, communities, and customers. Those relationships act as a cushion during times of uncertainty. Furthermore, businesses that contribute fairly to taxes help build infrastructure and services that benefit everyone. Roads, hospitals, schools, and a functioning social system create a stable environment in which businesses can operate and thrive.

When businesses take a broader view and recognize the importance of fairness, equity, and responsibility, it fosters a culture of innovation. The problems of the world, climate change, healthcare, poverty, and inequality, require innovative solutions, and those solutions are best found when people are motivated and have the resources they need to succeed. Canada, with its strong social infrastructure, has the opportunity to lead in these areas, and its corporate sector can play a vital role. By focusing on socially responsible practices, businesses can become part of the solution, driving the country forward and contributing to a healthier, more sustainable world.

The Financial Security Of Canadian Workers

Fair wages are an essential part of ensuring that Canadian workers feel financially secure and valued. When employees are paid a fair and livable wage, it provides them with the peace of mind that they can take care of their basic needs like housing, food, and healthcare without constantly stressing over how to make ends meet. This financial security is incredibly important because it allows workers to focus on their jobs, their families, and their personal well-being, rather than worrying about whether they'll be able to pay their bills next month. When people feel secure in their financial situation, it creates a sense of stability in their lives, which leads to a more positive and productive workforce.

Fair wages also foster job satisfaction. Workers who feel they are compensated fairly for their time and effort are more likely to feel motivated and engaged in their work. They are more likely to put in the extra effort and care about the quality of what they do because they know their work is valued. This creates a better overall work environment where people are more willing to collaborate, contribute ideas, and go above and beyond their basic responsibilities. Job satisfaction is closely tied to retention as well. When employees are paid well and feel their work is valued, they are more likely to stay with the company for the long term, reducing turnover and the costs associated with hiring and training new staff.

On top of job satisfaction, fair wages contribute to workers' well-being. A fair paycheck reduces stress and anxiety, especially for individuals who might otherwise be living paycheck to paycheck. When people aren't constantly concerned about their financial future, they are better able to focus on their personal health, maintain positive relationships, and invest in their futures. Employees who feel well-supported and financially secure are less likely to suffer from burnout, stress-related illnesses, or depression, which in turn lowers absenteeism and improves overall morale. A healthy, happy workforce is one that is more likely to show up, work hard, and produce high-quality results.

When people are financially secure, they also have the freedom to invest in their personal development. They can pursue education and training to improve their skills, learn new things, and grow within their field. This, in turn, leads to better productivity at work. Employees who have the ability to develop professionally are more likely to take on challenging tasks and innovate. As they become more skilled and knowledgeable, they become more valuable to their employers and to the economy as a whole. Fair wages, by promoting financial security, well-being, and job satisfaction, create a cycle of productivity that benefits everyone, not just the workers themselves but also the companies they work for and the broader Canadian economy.

A Strong Middle Class

Fair wages are one of the most important building blocks for creating a strong middle class, and when that middle class is thriving, it plays a critical role in strengthening national economic stability. When people are paid well enough to live comfortably and have some discretionary income, they are more likely to participate in the economy by purchasing goods and services. This drives demand, which in turn stimulates business growth and creates more job opportunities. A strong middle class essentially acts as the backbone of the economy, providing steady consumer demand that keeps businesses running and the economy growing.

A healthy middle class also contributes to national economic stability because it helps balance out the economy. If wages are too low and a large portion of the population is living paycheck to paycheck, they are less likely to spend money on anything beyond the bare essentials. This limits the potential for economic growth because there's less demand for goods and services. On the flip side, when people in the middle class have more financial security, they have the freedom to spend more on discretionary items, invest in their futures, and contribute to the overall well-being of the economy. This steady consumer spending helps buffer the economy against external shocks, like recessions or trade disruptions.

The strength of the middle class also lies in its ability to maintain consumer purchasing power. When wages rise, people have more money to spend, which increases their ability to buy things like homes, cars, food, and even services like healthcare and education. This, in turn, creates a positive cycle where businesses see increased sales and, as a result, are more likely to invest in innovation, new products, and hiring more people. As more people are employed and their wages rise, the cycle continues, contributing to long-term growth and resilience.

At the same time, a strong middle class helps reduce income inequality, which has been linked to social and economic instability. When the income gap widens too much, it creates tension between different segments of society, leading to dissatisfaction and potential unrest. A fair wage structure helps ensure that people in the middle class have a decent standard of living, which in turn helps promote social stability and cohesion. By providing fair wages, Canada can ensure that the middle class remains strong, contributing to economic stability and a prosperous future for everyone, not just a select few.

The Role Of Taxation In Supporting Government Services

Taxation plays a crucial role in supporting the essential services and infrastructure that help maintain a healthy, functioning society. Without a strong tax base, it would be impossible to provide the kind of support that citizens need to thrive, especially when facing challenges like a trade war or economic downturn. Taxes are the primary way governments can fund things like roads, public transportation, education, healthcare, and social services. These are not just conveniences; they are the foundation of a stable society. When citizens pay taxes, they are investing in the systems that allow their communities to flourish, ensuring everyone has access to the resources they need to live well.

National infrastructure, which includes things like roads, bridges, energy systems, and public transportation, is critical for keeping the economy moving smoothly. Without proper roads or reliable energy, businesses would struggle to operate, and workers would have difficulty commuting. Taxes fund the maintenance and development of these systems, ensuring that they are up to date and able to support the demands of a growing economy. Investing in infrastructure also creates jobs, providing immediate employment opportunities while laying the groundwork for future economic growth. It's a long-term investment in the country's ability to remain competitive on the global stage.

Education is another area that relies heavily on tax revenue. Public education, from elementary schools to universities, needs funding to provide quality teaching and resources. When taxes are used to support education, it means more opportunities for Canadians to access quality learning and build skills that are essential for the workforce. An educated population is not only more productive but also more innovative, which is key to solving the country's problems and adapting to new challenges, like the ones posed by a trade war. When people have the tools to succeed, they are more likely to contribute positively to society and the economy.

Healthcare is another critical service that depends on taxation. Canada's healthcare system, which provides access to necessary medical care for all citizens regardless of income, is funded primarily through taxes. Without this funding, many Canadians would face barriers to necessary medical treatments, which would harm their well-being and make the economy less productive. In a time of crisis, like a pandemic or a trade war, a well-funded healthcare system can help mitigate the damage by providing the resources needed to respond quickly and effectively. It keeps the population healthy, which in turn keeps the workforce strong and the economy stable.

Social services, including things like unemployment benefits, housing assistance, and child care subsidies, are also supported through taxes. These services provide a safety net for Canadians who are struggling and help prevent the negative social effects of poverty. During times of economic instability, like a trade war, social services become even more important. They help cushion the blow for people who lose their jobs or face other hardships, ensuring that they can still meet their basic needs. This support allows people to get back on their feet and re-enter the workforce, ultimately benefiting the economy as a whole.

Taxes, when used effectively, are not just a way for the government to generate revenue; they are a way to invest in the collective well-being of the country. They provide the foundation for the infrastructure, services, and programs that allow Canadians to lead productive, healthy lives. This investment creates a resilient society, one that can withstand external pressures and continue to thrive in the face of challenges. By ensuring that the tax system is fair and that the funds are used wisely, we can build a stronger, more stable country that benefits everyone.

Fair Taxes From Corporations

air taxes from corporations are a key ingredient in creating a more sustainable and prosperous society. When corporations contribute fairly to the tax system, they help fund the public services and infrastructure that make our society work. These taxes support everything from education and healthcare to transportation and social safety nets, all of which benefit employees and employers alike. A healthy, educated, and well-supported workforce is essential for the long-term success of any business. When businesses pay their fair share, they are investing in the kind of environment where both their employees and the economy can thrive.

One of the most important ways fair corporate taxes contribute to prosperity is by reducing the need for public assistance. When businesses pay fair wages and taxes, it means that fewer people need to rely on government programs like unemployment benefits, housing assistance, or food banks. By supporting their employees properly, corporations can help reduce the burden on the social safety net, freeing up those resources for people who truly need them. This, in turn, creates a more efficient and sustainable system where public funds can be used where they are most needed, rather than propping up companies that aren't contributing enough to the system.

Corporations that pay fair taxes also help create a more balanced and stable economy. When businesses contribute fairly, they help ensure that the economy is not overly reliant on a small number of sectors or industries. This reduces the risk of economic instability because it creates a more diversified and resilient economy. A strong, diverse economy benefits everyone, from employees to business owners. When businesses thrive in a balanced economy, they create more job opportunities, higher wages, and better working conditions. A thriving workforce, in turn, means more consumers with money to spend, creating a positive feedback loop that benefits everyone.

Fair taxes also help businesses themselves by supporting the infrastructure and services they rely on to operate. For example, good roads, reliable public transportation, and a healthy population all contribute to a business's ability to function smoothly. When corporations pay their fair share, they are helping to ensure that these systems remain in place and continue to serve both businesses and workers. This makes it easier for companies to grow and succeed, creating a more stable business environment.

In addition, when corporations pay their fair taxes, they are investing in the future. Taxes support education and innovation, two key components of long-term economic growth. By ensuring that employees have access to good schools and training programs, businesses help to build a more skilled and knowledgeable workforce. This, in turn, helps create more opportunities for businesses to grow and develop new products or services. A well-educated workforce is essential for any company that wants to stay competitive, and the taxes businesses pay help make that possible.

Ultimately, fair taxes from corporations help create a more equitable society. When businesses pay their fair share, they contribute to the overall well-being of the community. This benefits everyone, from employees who have better job security and access to social services, to employers who operate in a more stable and prosperous economy. By paying fair taxes, businesses are not only helping to support the systems they rely on, but they are also playing a key role in building a society that works for everyone. A sustainable, prosperous society is one where everyone has the opportunity to succeed, and fair corporate taxes are an essential part of making that happen.

A Minimum Tax Rate

When it comes to taxation, one of the most important things for a country like Canada is ensuring that all businesses contribute their fair share. A minimum tax rate, such as 3.5% on revenue, or 12.5% on profit, or the standard method, whichever one is higher, would be a practical approach. The goal here is not just about fairness or giving the government more money to work with, but also about addressing some of the deeper issues that exist within the Canadian economy. There are industries that thrive by exploiting Canadian resources, labour, and consumer equity without giving much back. These are the predatory businesses that exist primarily to drain the country of its wealth without contributing to its long-term prosperity.

Businesses that operate in Canada, whether they are Canadian-owned or foreign corporations, should not be allowed to escape paying taxes simply because they've found loopholes or ways to shift profits to other countries with lower tax rates. This doesn't just impact the government's ability to fund public services like healthcare, education, and infrastructure. It also has long-term consequences for the economy and the social fabric of the nation. When businesses aren't paying their fair share, it places an unfair burden on individuals, particularly on working-class Canadians. This is especially concerning when we consider the predatory industries that rely on cheap labour, low wages, and the exploitation of Canadian workers.

By implementing a minimum tax rate, we can make sure that these companies pay something back to the Canadian public. It becomes a level playing field, where all businesses are held to the same standard and contribute to the broader goals of Canadian society. A flat rate ensures that companies aren't incentivized to avoid taxes through aggressive loopholes or complicated schemes. They would have to contribute based on their revenue or profits, whichever is higher, which would prevent them from exploiting weaknesses in the tax system. It also ensures that no matter what kind of business you run, you will pay a fair share, which helps balance the scales for the rest of the economy.

But it's not just about keeping businesses honest. It's also about reducing the impact of industries that seek to exploit the Canadian workforce. There are certain sectors that thrive by offering low-paying jobs, often with little to no benefits, and contributing very little to the country's economic growth. These industries often don't invest in innovation or long-term job creation but instead rely on a cheap, easily replaceable workforce. When businesses can avoid paying taxes or getting away with paying very little, they have no incentive to raise wages, improve working conditions, or invest in the communities they operate in. This sets up a cycle where workers are stuck in low-wage jobs and are unable to break free from poverty or financial instability.

By introducing a minimum tax rate, we are not only ensuring that businesses pay their fair share but also limiting the power of these predatory industries. It forces them to contribute to the public coffers, which can be used to fund public goods like education, healthcare, and social services. These are the areas that benefit everyone, especially low-income workers who rely on these services for their well-being. When businesses are taxed appropriately, the wealth that is extracted from Canadian labour and consumers is returned to the people through better social infrastructure.

Additionally, the introduction of a minimum tax would also give Canadian businesses a better chance to compete. When large corporations can skirt their tax obligations, it creates an uneven playing field where small and medium-sized businesses that are paying their taxes are at a disadvantage. Larger companies have more resources to avoid taxes, leaving the little guys with a higher tax burden. This not only harms the competitive landscape but also discourages innovation and investment in the Canadian market. By levelling the playing field, a minimum tax ensures that all businesses have to follow the same rules and contribute to the system that supports them.

It's important to remember that businesses benefit from operating in Canada. They use Canadian infrastructure, tap into Canadian labour, and profit from the Canadian consumer market. When businesses avoid taxes or contribute little to the country's economy, they are taking more than they give. A minimum tax rate would be a way to make sure that these businesses are giving back to the country that allows them to operate and profit. It's about ensuring that the system works for everyone, not just the corporations that can afford to skirt the rules. This way, Canada can build a stronger, more sustainable economy that benefits its workers, its businesses, and the broader society.

Fair Wages And Overall Public Health

When people earn fair wages, it has a direct impact on their access to healthcare and, by extension, their overall public health. Fair wages ensure that people have the financial means to take care of their health in ways that are often out of reach for those who are underpaid. If someone is struggling to make ends meet, they are less likely to have access to the kind of healthcare that can help them stay healthy. They may delay medical treatment, avoid preventative care, or skip out on necessary prescriptions because they simply cannot afford it. This creates a cycle where poor health leads to financial instability, and financial instability leads to poor health. When people earn fair wages, they are more able to prioritize their well-being and access the care they need, which creates a healthier population overall.

A healthier population benefits everyone, including the economy. When people can afford regular doctor's visits, medications, mental health care, and other health services, they are able to stay productive in their jobs and contribute to society in a meaningful way. The relationship between fair wages and access to healthcare is a key part of breaking the cycle of poverty and poor health. When wages are low, people are forced to make hard choices between paying for medical care and covering basic living expenses, which often leads to their health suffering. This increases the strain on the public healthcare system because people who don't seek treatment early enough end up needing more expensive care later. It's also harder for people to recover and get back to work if their health is poor, which affects their economic productivity.

With fair wages, workers are better able to access not just emergency care, but preventive care as well. Preventative care is essential for avoiding chronic conditions like diabetes, heart disease, and mental health struggles. People with fair wages are able to see their doctor regularly for check-ups, get vaccinated, and attend to health issues before they become more serious. This type of care helps people live longer, healthier lives and reduces the long-term costs of healthcare for both individuals and society. It can also create a more stable workforce, where people can continue to work and support themselves and their families without the added stress of poor health.

Another aspect of fair wages and public health is the connection to mental health. Financial stress can have a significant impact on a person's mental health, leading to anxiety, depression, and other mental health issues. When people are paid fairly, they don't have to constantly worry about their financial security, which gives them the mental space to focus on their overall well-being. Being able to afford mental health care, whether it's therapy, counselling, or support groups, is just as important as physical health care. When people are mentally healthy, they are more likely to stay engaged in their communities, succeed at work, and live a fulfilling life. This creates a stronger, more resilient society where everyone can thrive.

Fair wages also contribute to a sense of dignity and stability, which plays a huge role in people's overall health. When workers are compensated fairly, they feel valued and appreciated, which boosts their self-esteem and motivation. This sense of worth is tied to their well-being, as it gives them the confidence to seek out medical care when they need it, take time off work for recovery, and generally live a more balanced, healthier life. Fair wages provide people with the security they need to take care of themselves, knowing that they can afford the necessary resources without fear of falling behind financially.

In the end, fair wages and access to healthcare go hand in hand when it comes to public health. Fair wages allow people to access the care they need, whether that's physical, mental, or preventive health care. It also creates a healthier, more productive population, which benefits the economy and society as a whole. When people are paid fairly, they are healthier, happier, and more able to contribute to their communities. This is why fair wages should be seen not just as a moral issue, but as an investment in the health and well-being of the entire country.

Improved Worker Health And Well-Being

When workers are healthy and feel well-supported, they perform better across the board. It's a pretty simple equation; healthier workers are more productive. It's not just about physical health either. Mental health plays a huge role here. When people are feeling good, both physically and mentally, they can focus better, work harder, and stay engaged with what they're doing. That means they get more done in less time, which is a win for both the employee and the company they work for.

A healthy workforce also means fewer sick days. When people aren't constantly fighting off colds or dealing with stress-related illnesses, they show up to work more consistently. The fewer days employees take off, the less disruption there is to the flow of work. Not only does this improve the overall efficiency of a business, but it also saves the company money. Think about it—when employees call in sick, it doesn't just affect their workload; it often falls on others to pick up the slack, which can create even more stress and dissatisfaction.

Good health, along with feeling like they are being treated well, also boosts morale. Employees who are healthy and well taken care of feel more valued by their employers. When workers see that their well-being is a priority, they're more likely to stay motivated, work hard, and contribute ideas that drive the business forward. That kind of positive morale is contagious, too. It spreads throughout teams and departments, creating a workplace atmosphere that's conducive to collaboration and innovation. When people feel like they're part of a supportive team, they're more likely to stay engaged and keep pushing forward, even when things get tough.

On top of all that, healthier workers tend to have better relationships with their coworkers. A strong support system is key to good teamwork, and when people are healthy and feel cared for, they can communicate better and resolve conflicts more easily. This leads to a smoother workflow, where everyone is on the same page, working together toward common goals. When workplace morale is high, people are also more willing to go the extra mile to help each other out, which strengthens the overall performance of the company.

Ultimately, the connection between worker health, well-being, and productivity is undeniable. It's not just about giving people the tools they need to do their jobs; it's about giving them the space to thrive. When workers are treated well and supported in all aspects of their health, they bring their best selves to work, leading to a more efficient, happier, and productive workforce.

Health-Focused Approach To Corporate Policies

There are several countries around the world that have taken a health-focused approach to corporate policies, and the results speak for themselves. Look at places like Sweden and Germany, where companies prioritize the well-being of their workers, from providing generous health benefits to fostering a work-life balance that's part of the national culture. In these countries, workers aren't just seen as cogs in a machine; they are valued, and that has paid off in terms of both productivity and overall economic success. Companies in these countries tend to have lower turnover rates because workers are less stressed and feel supported. That means less time and money spent on recruiting and training new employees, and more stability for the business.

Take a look at the German model of co-determination, where workers have a say in how companies are run. It creates a more engaged workforce, and when workers have a voice, they are often more invested in the success of the company. That sense of shared responsibility leads to better decision-making and a more productive environment. It's not just about paying workers well or giving them benefits; it's about creating a company culture that values collaboration and well-being, which in turn fosters innovation and loyalty. Germany's approach has led to a strong economy, high levels of job satisfaction, and businesses that are more adaptable in times of economic challenge.

Then there's Japan, which has a long history of promoting employee health through government initiatives and corporate practices. The idea of "lifetime employment" in Japan is part of a larger focus on taking care of workers, which includes everything from regular health checks to access to quality healthcare. In return, companies benefit from workers who are healthier, stay longer with the company, and are more loyal. Japan has a highly skilled workforce, and that's partly because the health of its workers is seen as an asset. When workers are healthy, they can focus on learning, improving their skills, and staying productive, which keeps the country's industries competitive on the global stage.

Even in countries like Canada and the UK, where healthcare is more accessible, we see the positive effects of a health-focused policy on businesses. Companies that offer wellness programs, mental health support, and healthy working environments report better outcomes in terms of employee performance. For example, companies in the UK that offer flexible working hours or mental health days often see a reduction in absenteeism and an increase in overall productivity. Employees feel less pressure and more supported, which leads to a more sustainable workforce. These countries show us that a healthy workforce isn't just good for the individual; it's good for the economy as a whole.

The evidence is clear; when countries invest in the health and well-being of their workforce, they see improvements in productivity, job satisfaction, and overall economic stability. Industries that prioritize health-focused policies are often more innovative, adaptable, and resilient in the face of economic challenges. They create an environment where workers can thrive, which leads to long-term success for both employees and employers. These examples show that health is not just a benefit for individuals; it's an essential part of creating a thriving, competitive economy.

Resilience To Economic Disruption

A healthier workforce is undeniably a more resilient workforce, especially when it comes to weathering economic shocks and pandemics. When people are healthier, they are less likely to need frequent medical care, which means fewer absences from work and fewer burdens on the healthcare system. This translates to fewer people relying on public assistance, making the entire economy more stable. If workers are healthy, they can continue to contribute productively, which helps businesses stay afloat during tough times. If a company has a healthier workforce, it is more likely to keep running smoothly and keep people employed, which is a huge advantage during an economic downturn. On the other hand, when workers are unhealthy, whether from chronic illnesses, mental health challenges, or inadequate healthcare, they're more likely to fall behind in the workforce. This leads to reduced productivity, increased absenteeism, and in some cases, layoffs. The financial strain then ripples outward, as businesses may need to rely on social programs to support their employees, further draining public resources.

Looking at pandemics, the connection becomes even clearer. A workforce that is healthier overall is better able to withstand the physical, emotional, and economic challenges of a pandemic. Workers who have access to good healthcare, who are in good physical condition, and who are supported in maintaining their well-being will be less likely to experience severe health consequences if they are exposed to a virus. This reduces the number of people who need long-term care, which in turn eases the pressure on hospitals, healthcare workers, and the public health system. A healthier workforce can adapt more quickly to changes in the economy during a crisis because they are less likely to be sidelined by illness or exhaustion. If the pandemic hits, people can work remotely or take on new roles more easily, keeping the economy moving even during times of disruption.

The financial burden of a workforce that is not healthy is enormous. When people get sick, they often need more than just time off work; they may require medical treatment, pharmaceuticals, and long-term care, all of which are expensive and place a strain on government resources. The financial burden then extends beyond the healthcare system to affect all public services, like social security or unemployment benefits, which are meant to support people when they're out of work. If fewer people need assistance because they are healthier, then the entire system works more efficiently. It also means that more workers can continue paying taxes and contributing to social programs, which helps support the system as a whole.

On top of that, a healthier workforce has more confidence in the future, and people who feel secure in their health are more likely to spend money, invest in the economy, and participate in society at large. When people are constantly worrying about their health or their ability to access healthcare, it creates a drag on consumer spending and confidence. A workforce that is strong and healthy creates an environment of stability. A healthy society is an economically productive society, and when businesses and workers are healthy, they are much more likely to thrive even when the world around them is in turmoil. The bottom line is simple: healthier workers are better for everyone, including businesses, governments, and the economy at large.

Employee Education, Training, And Skill Development

Corporate social responsibility (CSR) goes beyond simply being good to the environment or donating to charity; it involves a deeper commitment to improving the communities that businesses operate within, and this includes investing in their employees' education, training, and skill development. Canadian companies can play a key role in helping workers stay ahead of the curve when it comes to technological advancements and the evolving demands of the job market. By investing in their employees' skills, businesses are not just helping individual workers, but they are also strengthening their organizations and the broader economy.

In a world where technology and industries are constantly changing, workers need to adapt to stay relevant. The pace of change in fields like automation, artificial intelligence, and renewable energy is accelerating, and companies need to be proactive in preparing their employees for these shifts. Canadian businesses can take the lead by providing continuous learning opportunities for their workforce. This can mean offering on-the-job training programs, funding for continuing education, or partnerships with educational institutions to create pathways for skill development. When employees are equipped with the skills they need, businesses benefit from a more capable, agile workforce that can handle new challenges and drive innovation.

Companies also need to support vocational training programs that focus on the practical, hands-on skills that are necessary in a variety of industries, especially in sectors like manufacturing, construction, and technology. Not everyone is going to pursue a four-year degree, and that's where vocational training comes in. These programs focus on equipping workers with the specific skills they need for their job roles, and they can be especially helpful in industries where there is a skills gap. A focus on skill development allows workers to grow in their careers, while businesses can be confident they have the talent they need to stay competitive in the market.

For Canadian businesses, investing in education and training can also help meet future industrial needs. As new technologies emerge, there will be new demands for skilled workers. By prioritizing employee training now, companies can ensure they have the talent they need for the future. This kind of long-term investment helps businesses stay ahead of competitors who may be slower to adapt. It's an investment that not only benefits workers but also creates a more resilient, forward-thinking workforce that can address the challenges of tomorrow.

Supporting educational initiatives goes beyond internal training programs. Canadian businesses can collaborate with schools, colleges, and universities to create specialized training courses and curriculum that address current and future industry needs. This could mean supporting STEM programs in schools, funding scholarships for students pursuing tech-related degrees, or partnering with vocational schools to develop customized training for specific industries. When companies invest in education on a larger scale, they help create a pipeline of talented workers who are ready to take on the jobs of the future.

The truth is, the workforce of the future needs to be adaptable, skilled, and prepared for change. By investing in education and training, Canadian companies not only help their employees grow, but they also create a more dynamic, innovative, and capable workforce that can meet the demands of a rapidly changing world. This is the kind of proactive strategy that can ensure Canada remains competitive on the global stage while providing valuable opportunities for workers.

Impact Of Education On Productivity And Innovation

Education plays a fundamental role in shaping the productivity and innovation of any workforce. A well-educated workforce is more capable of tackling complex challenges, developing new ideas, and adapting quickly to changes in the economy. With global markets shifting constantly, whether it's due to technological advancements, political shifts, or new economic challenges, having workers who are educated and skilled is more crucial than ever. When people are equipped with the right knowledge and tools, they can respond to change more effectively, find innovative solutions to problems, and ultimately contribute to the long-term economic success of their country.

A highly skilled workforce can drive productivity across every sector of the economy. When workers have access to solid education, they develop not just specific technical skills, but also critical thinking, problem-solving abilities, and the capacity to learn and adapt to new situations. These qualities are invaluable, particularly in today's economy where change is constant and rapid. The more educated a worker is, the more productive they can be in their role. Whether it's in manufacturing, technology, or healthcare, having workers who understand the nuances of their field allows for more efficient processes, better decision-making, and higher overall output.

But it's not just about being productive today; it's about being prepared for the future. With the rapid rise of automation, artificial intelligence, and other technological advancements, workers need to be able to adapt to these new tools and systems. A well-educated workforce is better positioned to understand and integrate these changes, ensuring that industries stay competitive on a global scale. Workers who are trained in emerging technologies, for example, can help businesses adopt new systems quickly, improving efficiency and keeping companies ahead of competitors who may be slower to adapt. Education in these areas doesn't just help individuals stay relevant, but it helps entire industries remain strong and viable in a fast-moving world.

In the long run, investing in education creates an economic environment where innovation can thrive. A highly educated workforce is not only better at responding to immediate challenges, but it also drives the creative thinking that leads to new industries and breakthroughs. Countries that prioritize education often find themselves at the forefront of innovation, developing new technologies, services, and ideas that can shape global markets. By having a workforce that is adaptable and capable of thinking outside the box, businesses are able to stay competitive, and the entire economy benefits from the wealth of new ideas and products that emerge from this innovative thinking.

The long-term economic benefits of an educated workforce are clear. Economies that invest in education see improved economic growth, higher levels of income, and reduced inequality. Education leads to higher levels of job satisfaction, better wages, and greater opportunities for workers. On a broader scale, having a workforce that is well-educated and highly skilled means that the economy is more resilient to external shocks, whether from global recessions, pandemics, or geopolitical conflicts. The ability of a country's workers to innovate and adapt ensures that it can weather these challenges and come out stronger on the other side.

In today's interconnected world, no country can afford to fall behind when it comes to education. As industries evolve, workers need to evolve with them. A highly educated and adaptable workforce isn't just an asset for individuals, it's an asset for the whole economy. When people are prepared to tackle the challenges of the future, they contribute to a stronger, more competitive economy that can stand its ground in the global marketplace.

Socially Responsible Companies Create A Culture Of Innovation

When companies prioritize social responsibility, they set the stage for a culture of innovation. Focusing on fair wages, employee well-being, and education doesn't just create a positive work environment; it sparks creativity and new ideas. Fair wages ensure that employees are financially secure, reducing stress and allowing them to focus on their work rather than worrying about making ends meet. This security fosters a sense of loyalty and investment in the company's mission, which in turn drives people to think outside the box and contribute their best ideas. Employees who are well-compensated feel valued and are more likely to go the extra mile in finding creative solutions and improving processes.

Well-being is just as crucial when it comes to creating an innovative culture. When companies take care of their employees' mental and physical health, they are more likely to see a positive impact on performance. Employees who feel healthy, supported, and appreciated are not only more engaged in their work, but they are also more likely to come up with innovative ideas. Well-being initiatives, whether through health programs, flexible work options, or a positive work-life balance, create a space where employees can thrive. This environment makes them feel empowered to take risks and try new approaches, which is essential for innovation. A happy and healthy workforce is more productive, and that productivity is often channelled into creative problem-solving.

Education plays a huge role in fostering innovation within a company. By investing in ongoing employee education and training, businesses ensure that their workforce is always learning and adapting. As industries evolve, so too must the people within them. When companies provide opportunities for skill development and offer training in emerging technologies, they not only equip employees with the tools they need to excel but also encourage them to think creatively. Education expands people's thinking and exposes them to new ideas and concepts that they can bring into their work. When employees are constantly learning, they are more likely to identify areas for improvement and propose new ways of doing things.

All of this creates a work culture where innovation can flourish. When employees feel secure in their jobs, healthy in their bodies and minds, and constantly challenged to learn and grow, they are in the ideal mindset to innovate. They have the resources, support, and freedom to think creatively, take risks, and contribute ideas that might have otherwise been overlooked. Companies that focus on social responsibility are investing in the future, not just of their employees, but of their business as well. By cultivating a culture where people are encouraged to innovate, these companies set themselves up for long-term success, creating products, services, and solutions that are ahead of the curve. This type of environment not only leads to growth but also helps businesses stay competitive in a rapidly changing market. When companies focus on their people, the results are clear: innovation, growth, and a thriving business.

Investing In Research And Development

Investing in research and development (R&D) is crucial for companies that want to stay ahead in an increasingly competitive and fast-changing world. It is about more than just creating new products or improving existing ones. It is about creating an environment where employees are encouraged to think critically and contribute to finding solutions, not just for their business but for the challenges facing both Canada and the world. R&D is the backbone of innovation. When companies invest in R&D, they are giving themselves the tools to respond to shifting markets, changing consumer demands, and global issues. A company that makes R&D a priority is showing that it values creativity, forward-thinking, and solving real-world problems, which ultimately leads to growth, both financially and in terms of impact.

The benefits of investing in R&D go beyond just having a competitive edge. R&D allows companies to be more adaptable. In today's world, problems can arise unexpectedly, whether it's a global pandemic, environmental disaster, or a shift in consumer behaviour. Companies that have a strong foundation in R&D are better positioned to quickly pivot and respond to these challenges. When employees are given the freedom to experiment, learn, and develop new ideas, they are not only advancing the company but also contributing to solving the bigger problems. Encouraging a culture of critical thinking in the workplace empowers employees to tackle issues from multiple angles, bringing fresh perspectives that are necessary for finding innovative solutions.

Looking at Canadian companies, we can see clear examples of how focusing on innovation, sustainability, and problem-solving has helped businesses thrive. Take Bombardier, for example. Their investment in R&D has made them a leader in the aviation and transportation sectors, with cutting-edge technology that continues to drive global innovation. While their journey has been complex, their ongoing commitment to R&D has enabled them to maintain a presence in a highly competitive industry. Another great example is Shopify. As a company that started small, Shopify has leveraged R&D and technological innovation to become one of the world's leading e-commerce platforms. By continually evolving and enhancing its platform, Shopify has been able to solve critical problems for entrepreneurs and businesses, especially during challenging times like the COVID-19 pandemic. Their focus on innovation has made them a go-to solution for anyone looking to run an online business.

Then there's the renewable energy sector. Canadian companies like Brookfield Renewable Partners and Innergex have capitalized on the growing demand for clean energy. Their focus on sustainability, powered by heavy investments in R&D, has enabled them to develop renewable energy projects that are not only profitable but also contribute positively to the global effort against climate change. This kind of thinking isn't just good for the planet; it's good for business too. By staying at the forefront of renewable energy, these companies are building a sustainable future for themselves and others, creating solutions to one of the world's most pressing challenges while also positioning themselves as leaders in an evolving market.

What all of these companies have in common is their focus on innovation and problem-solving. They understand that R&D isn't just an expense, it's an investment in the future. By creating environments where employees are encouraged to think critically and come up with new ideas, they're positioning themselves not only for success in the marketplace but for long-term relevance. It's about recognizing that the problems we face today, whether local or global, require creative solutions, and the companies that foster a culture of innovation are the ones that will be best equipped to create those solutions.

Tangible Solutions To Difficult Problems

When companies focus on innovation, the benefits stretch far beyond just making a profit. Sure, businesses that prioritize innovation can create products and services that make them more competitive, but they can also be part of something much bigger. Innovation is not just about selling more; it's about solving the problems that matter most to society. Take climate change, for example. Businesses that invest in developing new technologies or systems that reduce environmental harm are contributing directly to one of the most pressing global issues. Whether it's renewable energy sources, sustainable agriculture practices, or carbon capture technologies, companies that innovate in these areas are helping to create a more sustainable world. By focusing on making these solutions more efficient, affordable, and accessible, these companies are not only doing the right thing but also tapping into new markets, boosting profitability, and securing their future as global leaders in sustainability.

Healthcare is another area where innovation can drive real change. We've seen incredible breakthroughs in medicine and technology over the past few decades, from better diagnostic tools to treatments for previously untreatable diseases. Companies that invest in healthcare innovation can help make these advancements more accessible, especially in countries where healthcare systems are under pressure or where access to treatment is limited. Whether it's through telemedicine, improved health data analytics, or more affordable pharmaceuticals, businesses can play a critical role in ensuring that healthcare reaches more people, more efficiently. What's important here is that these innovations do not just improve the well-being of individuals but also reduce the overall burden on the healthcare system, saving money and making it easier for governments and businesses alike to ensure that health services are more equitable and far-reaching.

Social inequality is another area where innovation can make a tangible difference. Companies that develop products or services aimed at improving the lives of disadvantaged communities, whether through affordable housing, access to education, or financial inclusion, can help to bridge the gap between the haves and the have-nots. By focusing on inclusivity and using innovation to solve problems like lack of access to education or fair wages, businesses can empower individuals who have historically been marginalized. This is where innovation intersects with social responsibility. Companies that focus on solving social problems through innovative solutions not only make a difference in people's lives, but they also create new opportunities for growth and profit. For example, tech companies are increasingly developing affordable, scalable educational tools that help people in remote areas gain access to learning, breaking down barriers that would have previously made it impossible for many to get an education.

In all these cases, innovation drives profitability, but it also helps companies solve real-world problems that matter to society. Businesses that invest in creating solutions to climate change, healthcare access, and social inequality are not just doing good work; they are also positioning themselves as leaders in industries that will be essential for the future. As society faces increasingly complex challenges, companies that innovate are the ones that can provide the answers, securing their place in the market while also making a lasting impact. By focusing on solving these issues, businesses create a cycle of improvement where their success directly contributes to broader social, economic, and environmental well-being. This, in turn, ensures that the benefits of innovation extend far beyond the walls of the company itself, creating a ripple effect that can be felt in every corner of society.

Resistance To Economic Disruption

When companies create a socially responsible corporate environment, it's not just about doing the right thing for employees or the environment; it also makes good business sense, especially when you look at the long-term stability of the company. In times of economic pressures like global trade wars, recessions, or supply chain disruptions, businesses that focus on socially responsible practices tend to fare better. Take stable wages, for example. Companies that provide fair pay create a workforce that is more engaged and productive. Workers who are paid well are less likely to leave their jobs or become disengaged, meaning that companies avoid the costs associated with high turnover or the negative effects of a dissatisfied workforce. In addition, when people are paid fairly, they have more disposable income, which in turn supports local economies. This creates a more stable customer base for companies, as people are more likely to spend money on products or services when they feel financially secure.

Another aspect of a socially responsible corporate environment is local production. Companies that focus on producing goods locally, or within regions that have stable and reliable supply chains, are less susceptible to the kinds of global disruptions that can wreck havoc on international trade. For example, during trade wars or when supply chains break down, businesses that rely on international imports for key parts or raw materials can quickly face delays, higher costs, or even shortages. Companies that produce goods locally or source materials from nearby suppliers are in a much stronger position to weather these disruptions because they aren't as reliant on the instability of far-flung global markets. This local approach not only reduces dependence on external factors but also supports local economies, creating a win-win situation for both companies and the surrounding communities.

Sustainable business practices are another key factor in creating resilience against economic pressures. Companies that invest in sustainability, whether through energy-efficient technologies, waste reduction, or ethical sourcing of materials, are better positioned to ride out the ups and downs of global markets. For one, sustainability often leads to cost savings over time. For example, by reducing waste and energy consumption, businesses can lower their operating costs, which can help protect them against rising prices or supply chain disruptions. Moreover, businesses that practice sustainability are increasingly seen as responsible corporate citizens, which can build consumer trust and loyalty. In a time when environmental concerns are top of mind for many people, companies that take sustainability seriously are not just protecting the planet; they're also protecting their brand reputation and securing long-term customer loyalty.

By focusing on these key areas, stable wages, local production, and sustainable business practices, companies make themselves more resilient in the face of external economic pressures. Stable wages create a loyal and productive workforce, local production shields companies from global supply chain disruptions, and sustainability makes businesses more competitive while protecting them against unpredictable market shifts. When companies adopt these practices, they build not just a better business model but a stronger foundation that can weather any economic storm. By investing in their people, communities, and the environment, socially responsible companies set themselves up for success, even when the global economy is anything but predictable. This kind of resilience isn't just good for the company; it's good for the entire economy, making sure that everyone benefits from more sustainable and reliable business practices.

Industry Resilience

When industries focus on resilience by prioritizing fair wages, sustainable practices, and robust worker support, they tend to be much better equipped to handle external economic shocks than those focused solely on short-term profits. The reason for this is simple: resilience comes from building strong foundations, and those foundations are rooted in people, practices, and long-term thinking. Companies that pay fair wages create a stable workforce. Workers who are paid fairly are more likely to stay with the company, feel valued, and stay engaged with their work. This creates a sense of stability within the company, and stability in the workforce translates to more consistency in productivity. In times of economic downturn, companies with loyal employees are better positioned to maintain operations and weather the storm, while businesses that constantly push for lower wages or temporary cost-cutting measures risk losing their most skilled workers and facing high turnover, which can be disruptive and costly.

Sustainable practices also play a crucial role in resilience. Industries that focus on sustainability are less vulnerable to the fluctuations of global markets and supply chains. For example, a company that invests in renewable energy or energy-efficient technologies may have higher initial costs, but these investments pay off in the long run. They lower operating costs, reduce dependence on volatile energy markets, and make the company more self-sufficient. On the other hand, companies that prioritize short-term profit maximization often cut corners when it comes to sustainability, which can lead to higher long-term costs. These companies may find themselves at a disadvantage when regulations change, or when the cost of raw materials or energy increases. Sustainability is an investment in the future, and industries that ignore this are often less equipped to cope with changing market dynamics.

Another key aspect of resilience is robust worker support. Companies that provide strong support for their employees, whether through healthcare, mental health resources, or career development opportunities, tend to have a workforce that is more adaptable and willing to stick with the company when times get tough. Workers who feel supported and valued are more likely to go the extra mile when needed. They are also more resilient themselves, able to handle stress or uncertainty with more grace. In contrast, companies that don't invest in their people, focusing only on short-term profits, often find that their workforce is less committed and more prone to burnout. When economic shocks hit, these businesses may struggle with low morale, high turnover, and disengagement, which can leave them ill-prepared to recover.

Industries that take the long-term view, those that focus on creating value for their employees, customers, and the environment, are far more resilient to external shocks. They aren't looking for a quick fix or a temporary boost. Instead, they're building a foundation that can adapt to changing circumstances. When a crisis happens, whether it's a trade war, a recession, or a global pandemic, these industries are in a better position to continue functioning, because they've already created systems that allow them to be flexible and sustainable. In contrast, industries that focus solely on short-term profits may look good for a time, but they're often too fragile to withstand the kinds of shocks that are inevitable in any economy. They may prioritize shareholder returns over long-term sustainability, but in the end, it's the businesses that focus on resilience that come out ahead. By creating fair wages, sustainable practices, and strong worker support systems, industries not only protect themselves from the worst of economic shocks but also build the kind of lasting value that will carry them through whatever comes next.

Global Pressure To Meet Ethical Standards

Canadian corporations face growing global pressure to meet ethical standards, especially when it comes to human rights, environmental protection, and equitable business practices. As the world becomes more interconnected, there is increasing scrutiny on how businesses operate, not just locally, but on a global scale. Human rights are no longer just a matter of domestic policy; they are a critical factor in how companies are perceived and how they interact with international markets. Environmental concerns have also risen to the forefront, with many consumers, investors, and governments demanding that companies take responsibility for their carbon footprint and overall environmental impact. On top of that, there's an expectation for businesses to be fair in their practices, whether it's in their treatment of employees, their supply chains, or their efforts to combat inequality.

Canada has the opportunity to take the lead in setting high standards for ethically responsible business practices. We've always been known for our commitment to fairness, justice, and environmental stewardship. By reinforcing these values, Canadian businesses can show the world that it's possible to be profitable while being socially responsible. Businesses here can take proactive steps to ensure they are protecting human rights, advocating for fair labour practices, and investing in environmental sustainability. They can make sure their supply chains are transparent and free from exploitation, especially in developing countries, which is a growing concern for consumers who are becoming more conscious of the global impact of their purchasing choices.

One way Canada can lead the way is by incentivizing businesses to adopt green technologies and more sustainable practices. Rather than waiting for external pressures or regulations to force companies to change, Canadian businesses could take the initiative to implement renewable energy solutions, reduce waste, and promote circular economies. Environmental protection isn't just a moral obligation; it's also a practical business strategy that can lead to long-term savings and a stronger market position as consumers increasingly prioritize sustainability.

When it comes to equitable business practices, Canada has the chance to foster a more inclusive and fair business environment. There is a growing demand for diversity, equity, and inclusion in the workplace, and Canadian companies can set a strong example by ensuring fair treatment for all employees, regardless of background or gender. This would also extend to how businesses approach their relationships with Indigenous communities, racial minorities, and other historically marginalized groups. By promoting an inclusive environment where everyone has equal access to opportunities, Canadian companies can show that businesses can grow and succeed while embracing diversity.

Canada can also encourage ethical business practices by establishing government incentives, regulations, and standards that align with these values. By setting the bar high in terms of human rights, environmental protection, and equitable practices, the country can set the standard for other nations and industries to follow. Rather than reacting to global trends, Canada can become a proactive leader that shapes these trends. Through international collaborations, investments in sustainable technologies, and commitments to human rights, Canadian businesses can inspire others to adopt similar practices and make a real difference in the world.

In doing so, Canada would not only protect its own industries from the risks of unethical business practices but also strengthen its reputation as a global leader in socially responsible business. It can shift the narrative away from corporate greed and exploitation to one of fairness, sustainability, and progress. Canadian companies that rise to meet these ethical standards can create a ripple effect that inspires global industries to prioritize the well-being of people and the planet over short-term profits, pushing the world toward a more just and sustainable future.

Addressing Global Challenges

Canadian companies have a unique opportunity to step up and lead by example in addressing some of the world's biggest challenges, like climate change, poverty, and inequality. These issues are no longer something that can be solved solely by governments or international organizations. It's clear that businesses play a huge role in shaping the future of our planet and society. Companies that actively engage in socially responsible actions do more than just contribute to solving these problems; they position themselves as leaders in a world that increasingly values sustainability, fairness, and integrity.

Take climate change as an example. We know that industries are some of the biggest contributors to carbon emissions and environmental degradation. But companies that are serious about reducing their carbon footprints can make a real impact. Whether it's by adopting renewable energy sources, improving energy efficiency, or shifting to sustainable practices in production and supply chains, Canadian companies can play a crucial role in reducing global greenhouse gas emissions. It's not just about saving the environment for the sake of it; it's also about future-proofing businesses. As governments worldwide tighten environmental regulations and consumers become more eco-conscious, companies that are ahead of the curve will find themselves in a better position to thrive. They can avoid costly fines and penalties and even benefit from incentives for sustainable practices.

Poverty and inequality are just as important, and businesses have the power to address these issues through fair wages, ethical supply chains, and promoting inclusion. By offering fair compensation and ensuring that workers have safe and healthy working conditions, companies can lift up entire communities. Many Canadian companies already do this, creating a positive ripple effect that extends beyond their employees to the wider economy. By focusing on fair wages, businesses help reduce poverty and ensure that people have the means to support their families, which in turn creates a stronger and more stable economy. Companies that make inclusion a priority, whether through hiring practices or offering equal opportunities for advancement, also contribute to narrowing the inequality gap. These companies are making a stand that every worker, no matter their background or identity, deserves to be treated with dignity and respect.

The great thing about companies that prioritize these values is that they are better positioned to attract global talent. People today are more selective about where they work. The younger generations, in particular, are drawn to companies that reflect their own values, particularly when it comes to sustainability and social responsibility. If a company is known for its commitment to tackling climate change, addressing inequality, and ensuring fair wages for its workers, it becomes a magnet for talent from around the world. Top-tier professionals want to work for companies that align with their beliefs, and by fostering a culture of integrity, these companies ensure they can attract and retain the best.

The same goes for investment. Investors are increasingly looking for companies that offer not just good returns but also contribute to the greater good. There's a growing emphasis on socially responsible investing, where funds are directed towards companies that have a positive impact on society and the environment. Canadian companies that are seen as leaders in social responsibility stand to benefit from increased investment, as investors know they are backing businesses that are future-focused and ethically driven. These companies also benefit from a growing customer base that cares about sustainability. As consumers become more aware of the impact their purchasing decisions have on the world, they increasingly seek out brands that share their values. Companies that make a clear commitment to socially responsible actions, from reducing their carbon footprint to ensuring fair wages, stand out in a crowded market and attract customers who are loyal to brands that reflect their own values.

In a world where sustainability, fairness, and integrity are becoming the gold standard, Canadian companies that embrace these principles are not only doing the right thing—they're setting themselves up for long-term success. These companies attract the best talent, earn the trust of consumers, and stand out to investors. Most importantly, they contribute to addressing the global challenges we face today, making the world a better place in the process.

Government And Corporate Social Responsibility

The government plays a critical role in encouraging corporate social responsibility (CSR) by creating an environment where companies are motivated to do the right thing. It's not just about asking businesses to be ethical or to make responsible choices; it's about setting up the right framework that aligns social good with business success. One way the government can do this is through regulation, making sure that companies meet certain standards when it comes to fair wages, taxes, and sustainability. But regulation alone doesn't always do the trick. It's also important for governments to create incentives and offer support, encouraging businesses to go beyond the bare minimum and invest in the long-term health of society and the environment.

Regulation is essential because it sets the baseline for what is acceptable and what isn't. Without it, some companies might prioritize short-term profits over their responsibilities to workers, communities, and the planet. For example, setting minimum wage laws ensures that businesses can't exploit workers by paying them too little, while regulations on tax compliance ensure that corporations contribute their fair share to public services and infrastructure. Governments can also enforce environmental regulations that limit pollution and waste, making it clear that businesses need to take responsibility for their environmental impact. But these regulations don't need to be heavy-handed or punitive; they can be designed to guide businesses toward better practices without stifling innovation or growth. By ensuring that everyone follows the same rules, governments can level the playing field and encourage businesses to adopt CSR as part of their core operations.

Incentives are another key piece of the puzzle. Companies are more likely to adopt CSR practices if there's something in it for them, and governments can provide these incentives in several ways. Tax breaks are one of the most common tools. If a company reduces its carbon footprint, invests in renewable energy, or pays fair wages to its employees, the government can offer tax incentives or deductions. This not only helps businesses save money but also encourages them to prioritize these practices. Other incentives could include access to government contracts for companies that meet certain CSR criteria. If a company wants to bid on a government project, for example, they might need to demonstrate that they are contributing to social good, paying their fair share of taxes, and following sustainable practices. This creates a competitive advantage for businesses that are serious about CSR, making it more attractive for them to engage in these responsible practices.

Support is also vital. While regulation and incentives can drive change, governments can go a step further by providing support to help businesses transition to more socially responsible models. This could include grants for research and development into sustainable technologies or programs that help small businesses implement CSR strategies. Governments can also provide educational resources and training to help businesses understand the benefits of CSR and how to implement it effectively. This kind of support allows businesses to see CSR not as a burden but as an opportunity to grow, innovate, and strengthen their position in the market.

A potential policy framework that could encourage corporations to adopt fair wages, fair taxes, and sustainable practices might start with clear, enforceable regulations that set the minimum expectations for all companies. These could include basic standards for wages, environmental impact, and tax contributions. Beyond that, governments could create a tiered system where businesses that go above and beyond those basic standards are rewarded with financial incentives or special recognition. For example, a company that implements zero-waste practices or reduces its carbon emissions by a certain percentage could receive tax breaks or access to low-interest loans for further sustainability initiatives. At the same time, businesses that fail to meet these standards could face penalties, like fines or reduced access to government contracts.

In addition, the government could partner with the private sector to foster innovation. By providing funding for green technologies, sustainable agriculture practices, or workforce development programs, governments can help create the infrastructure that supports CSR. With this kind of backing, businesses can feel more confident in making long-term investments that benefit both their bottom line and society at large.

The key here is balance. Governments need to strike a careful balance between regulation, incentives, and support. If businesses feel like the government is putting too much pressure on them, they might resist or find ways to avoid compliance. But if there are too few regulations or incentives, companies might continue to cut corners. Governments need to create an environment where CSR is seen as both the right thing to do and a smart business strategy. This way, corporations will want to engage in socially responsible practices not just because they have to, but because it benefits them in the long run.

Government-Business Partnerships

When we talk about building a thriving economy, it's crucial to understand that it's not just about the government doing its part or businesses doing theirs. It's about the two working together. The government and businesses need to team up to create an environment where everyone benefits. When there's a strong partnership between them, the whole economy becomes stronger. It's not just the multinational corporations that gain, but also the smaller businesses and the communities they serve. A thriving economy isn't just about profits; it's about creating a system where businesses, workers, and communities all succeed together.

Governments have a unique position in this partnership because they have the ability to create policies and regulations that guide the way businesses operate. When governments design policies that encourage businesses to act responsibly, they set a foundation for growth that benefits everyone. For example, governments can create tax incentives for companies that prioritize sustainability, fair wages, and ethical practices. By doing this, they don't just punish bad behaviour; they actively reward businesses that make decisions with long-term positive impacts on society and the economy. But it's not just about incentives; it's about setting standards that hold businesses accountable. When governments create clear rules and regulations that focus on things like environmental protection, worker rights, and transparency, they help level the playing field and ensure that all businesses are working towards common, beneficial goals.

There are a number of successful examples from around the world where government-business partnerships have led to thriving, sustainable economies. Take the example of Denmark, where the government has played a critical role in shaping a green economy. The country has set ambitious goals for reducing carbon emissions and increasing the use of renewable energy. Danish businesses, particularly those in the wind energy sector, have flourished as a result. The Danish government not only sets regulations for sustainability but also provides support through subsidies and research grants to help businesses develop innovative solutions. This has turned Denmark into a global leader in wind energy, proving that when the government partners with businesses to meet shared goals, everyone can benefit. Businesses gain access to funding, technology, and a supportive regulatory environment, while the country moves towards a more sustainable, resilient economy.

Similarly, the Canadian government has provided examples of how partnerships with businesses can drive both social and economic progress. The Canadian government's investment in clean energy technologies and sustainable practices has encouraged businesses to innovate and adopt environmentally friendly practices. The government supports businesses that want to transition to greener models by offering tax incentives, grants, and access to clean energy programs. As a result, Canadian companies are leading in areas like clean tech and renewable energy, showing that when businesses and the government align their goals, they can contribute to both economic growth and sustainability.

Another example comes from the Japanese approach to corporate social responsibility. The Japanese government has long supported businesses in prioritizing long-term societal well-being over short-term profits. Through policies that promote worker rights, environmental protection, and community engagement, Japan has created a business culture that values responsibility. Companies that meet these standards are often rewarded with government contracts, tax breaks, and a strong reputation in the global marketplace. The close collaboration between government and businesses in Japan has helped create a robust, sustainable economy that focuses on both profit and social value.

In all these examples, the common thread is that when businesses and governments align their objectives, they create an economy that benefits everyone. Multinational corporations can thrive because they operate in a stable, predictable environment with clear regulations and incentives. Smaller businesses can also prosper because they are given the resources and support they need to grow and compete. Local communities benefit because businesses are encouraged to invest in sustainable practices and create jobs that support the well-being of workers. These partnerships ensure that the economy is not just growing but growing in a way that is inclusive and responsible.

For Canada, these global examples should serve as inspiration for what can be achieved through strong government-business partnerships. If Canada wants to remain competitive on the global stage, the government must continue to build policies that support responsible business practices. This includes not only incentivizing sustainability and fair labor practices but also ensuring that businesses contribute to the broader social good. When businesses are encouraged to think beyond profit and take responsibility for their environmental and social impact, they are better positioned to thrive in the long term. By aligning the goals of the government and businesses, we can create a more resilient, sustainable economy that benefits everyone, from local communities to multinational corporations.

Relationship Between Corporations And Society

Corporations and society have a deeply interconnected relationship. The success of one is tightly linked to the well-being of the other. It's not just about businesses profiting off of consumers, it's about businesses thriving because they are part of a functioning society that values fairness, responsibility, and sustainability. A corporation that is socially responsible isn't just thinking about how much money it can make. It is recognizing that its success is tied to the overall health of the community and the environment in which it operates. This is not just good for business, it's good for society too.

When a company prioritizes socially responsible practices, it does more than just improve its bottom line. It contributes to the broader social fabric. Social responsibility can take many forms: paying fair wages, offering benefits that support worker well-being, investing in local communities, adopting sustainable environmental practices, and ensuring that products are made ethically. Each of these elements is a way in which companies invest in society and create value that goes beyond financial returns. By doing so, businesses foster a sense of trust among the people they serve. When consumers see companies actively working for the betterment of society, they feel more confident in their choice to support those businesses. It builds social cohesion, bringing people together around shared values and a common sense of purpose.

A socially responsible corporate industry doesn't just contribute to economic growth; it actively helps reduce inequality. When companies pay fair wages and invest in workers' development, they create a more equitable society where everyone has a chance to improve their standard of living. This can help bridge the growing divide between the wealthy and the rest of the population. It also ensures that workers feel valued, which increases their productivity and overall happiness. In a society where more people feel economically secure, the risks of social unrest or resentment are lessened. Businesses that invest in reducing inequality are laying the groundwork for a more harmonious society, where the benefits of economic growth are shared more equally.

Public trust is another key area where socially responsible corporations make a difference. When businesses are transparent about their practices, commit to ethical standards, and show genuine concern for the public good, they build trust with their customers, employees, and the general public. Trust is the cornerstone of any successful business. Without it, people are less likely to support a company, less likely to buy its products, or work for it. A company that has earned public trust is one that has proven itself to be reliable, ethical, and committed to more than just its own profits. This level of trust helps stabilize not just individual companies, but entire industries. When trust is widespread, people feel more secure and are more willing to engage with the market in a positive way.

The relationship between corporations and society doesn't have to be a zero-sum game where businesses take as much as they can without considering the wider impact. When businesses focus on social responsibility, they recognize that their success is rooted in the health and prosperity of the communities they serve. The better those communities do, the better businesses will do. It's a mutually beneficial relationship that leads to greater economic growth, social stability, and a stronger sense of community. By fostering this symbiotic relationship, businesses contribute to a more sustainable and equitable world, where the benefits of growth are shared, trust is built, and inequality is reduced. It's a win-win for both corporations and society as a whole.

A Healthier Relationship Between Business And Society

When Canadian corporations invest in their workforce, by promoting health, education, and empowerment, it's not just a benefit for the workers themselves. It's an investment that ripples throughout the entire economy. A healthy and educated workforce is one that is more productive, more innovative, and more adaptable to changing market conditions. This means businesses can better weather economic shocks, adapt to new technologies, and keep up with global competition. When companies focus on ensuring their employees have the skills, training, and well-being to perform at their best, they set themselves up for long-term success.

But this doesn't just benefit the companies. It creates a more stable economy, which benefits everyone. Healthy employees are less likely to take sick days, are more engaged in their work, and contribute more to the overall productivity of the economy. An educated workforce, on the other hand, means that companies have access to workers who can solve complex problems and innovate in ways that keep industries competitive. When businesses make these kinds of investments, they are fostering a healthier economic environment where everyone is better positioned to succeed.

The benefits of this kind of workforce investment go beyond the balance sheets of individual corporations. When companies focus on the well-being and empowerment of their workers, it creates a positive feedback loop between business and the broader community. A prosperous economy depends on more than just businesses making profits. It requires people who are able to participate meaningfully in the economy, whether that means spending money, contributing ideas, or creating new businesses. A healthy, educated, and empowered workforce is a workforce that can contribute to a thriving economy, which in turn helps businesses grow and succeed.

When corporations align their success with the public good, they foster a relationship of mutual benefit. Workers who feel valued and supported by their employers are more likely to be loyal, productive, and innovative. They feel a connection to the company and are more motivated to contribute to its success. This sense of connection can also help build trust between businesses and the communities they operate in. A company that is seen as invested in its employees and their well-being is one that is more likely to earn the support of its customers, investors, and the general public. It becomes a business that people want to work for, invest in, and buy from.

This creates a positive cycle where businesses, workers, and the broader economy all benefit. A prosperous economy is one where businesses are thriving, workers are healthy and educated, and communities are stable and secure. When businesses invest in their workers and prioritize the public good, they create a more sustainable, resilient economy that benefits everyone involved. The relationship between business and society doesn't have to be adversarial or purely transactional. It can be a partnership where both sides work together to create long-term success. In the end, the healthier and more educated the workforce, the stronger and more prosperous the economy becomes. And when the economy is strong, businesses succeed, and society benefits.

Canadian Corporations Could Lead By Example

Imagine a future where Canadian corporations are seen as global leaders in fairness, sustainability, and innovation. These companies aren't just about making a profit; they're about creating long-term value for everyone involved. They set the standard for how businesses should operate, not just in Canada, but across the world. They show that being fair to workers, being mindful of the environment, and constantly seeking new ways to improve isn't just good for society; it's good for business.

In this future, businesses prioritize the health and well-being of their workers, paying fair wages, offering benefits that promote work-life balance, and creating safe environments where employees can thrive. They also invest in sustainable practices, reducing their environmental impact and ensuring their operations are as eco-friendly as possible. This isn't just about meeting regulations. It's about going above and beyond to make sure that businesses contribute positively to the world around them. And the result? A more stable, thriving economy where industries are built on principles of fairness and sustainability.

When Canadian companies adopt these values, the economy becomes stronger, more adaptable, and more resilient. By focusing on fairness and sustainability, businesses are less vulnerable to economic shocks, trade wars, and other external pressures. They are better equipped to weather challenges because they aren't constantly chasing short-term profits at the expense of long-term stability. Instead, they build businesses that are sustainable in every sense, economically, socially, and environmentally.

This kind of economy is one that attracts investment, talent, and global attention. Companies that lead by example become role models for others to follow. They attract customers who value sustainability and ethics, and investors who want to put their money into businesses that align with their values. Workers are drawn to these companies, knowing that they'll be treated fairly and given opportunities to grow. The economy as a whole benefits when businesses are focused on long-term success rather than short-term gains.

By adopting values of fairness, sustainability, and innovation, Canadian companies can create a future where businesses are not just competitive but are part of a larger movement toward a better global economy. This isn't about being at the forefront of a trend; it's about setting the standard for how businesses should function in the modern world. And as Canadian companies lead by example, the economy grows stronger and more resilient, making Canada an even more attractive place for investment, talent, and opportunity. In a rapidly changing global environment, Canada has the potential to show that businesses can thrive while also making the world a better place.

A Socially Responsible Corporate Sector Is A Practical Necessity

A socially responsible corporate sector isn't just about doing the right thing; it's about securing Canada's future. As the world changes, so too does the way businesses need to operate. More and more, the line between business success and social responsibility is blurring. Companies that focus on fairness, sustainability, and innovation aren't just contributing to a better society; they're positioning themselves for long-term success in a rapidly shifting global market.

In a world that increasingly values ethics, sustainability, and social good, businesses that ignore these priorities risk falling behind. The market isn't just about products and profits anymore. Consumers, investors, and employees are all paying attention to how companies treat their workers, how they manage their environmental impact, and whether they're contributing positively to the communities around them. If Canadian companies want to stay competitive and relevant on the world stage, they have to embrace these values, not just because it's the right thing to do, but because it's critical for long-term growth and stability.

Take a look at the big picture: a socially responsible corporate sector creates a more stable economy. When companies treat their workers fairly, pay decent wages, and invest in employee well-being, they create a healthier workforce that is more productive, more resilient, and more likely to stick around. When businesses embrace sustainable practices, they help protect the environment, reduce waste, and future-proof their operations. These efforts build trust with consumers and investors alike, fostering stronger, more reliable business relationships.

Canada's global standing is also tied to how its companies operate. A country known for leading with fairness, innovation, and sustainability is a country that earns respect on the world stage. In a time when global challenges like climate change, inequality, and health crises are front and centre, countries that prioritize these issues have a better chance of thriving. By investing in socially responsible businesses, Canada can demonstrate to the world that it's not just about economic growth; it's about responsible growth that takes into account the welfare of people, the planet, and future generations.

This is where the practical necessity of a socially responsible corporate sector becomes clear. Companies that don't adapt to this changing landscape risk being left behind. As global markets demand more ethical behaviour and sustainable practices, Canadian companies that don't keep up with these expectations will lose out on opportunities. The businesses that do embrace responsibility will attract investors, consumers, and workers who care about more than just the bottom line. And in turn, they'll drive Canada's long-term prosperity and bolster its reputation as a global leader.

Canada's future success, economically, socially, and politically, depends on how its corporate sector evolves. A strong, socially responsible corporate sector isn't just a moral imperative; it's essential for Canada's competitiveness and its ability to lead on the world stage. It's not just about being nice—it's about being smart, securing prosperity for future generations, and ensuring Canada remains relevant in the global economy.

Addressing The Affordability Crisis

The affordability crisis is something that's becoming impossible to ignore in Canada. Rising costs in almost every essential area, housing, food, healthcare, are making it harder for people to live comfortable, stable lives. When we look at housing, it's clear that many Canadians are being priced out of the market. Real estate prices, especially in major cities, have skyrocketed, and even with the best-paying jobs, owning a home is increasingly out of reach for the average person. Rent has also gone up, and people are feeling the squeeze as they try to make ends meet each month. For food, the story is similar. Grocery bills have gone through the roof, and families are having to cut back on what they can afford, which often means not getting the nutrition they need. Healthcare costs, too, have become a burden. While we have universal healthcare, things like dental care, prescription medications, and even some necessary medical treatments still come with high costs, creating additional stress for people who are already struggling financially.

It's important to note how the affordability gap is widening. It's not just about higher prices; it's about how these rising costs disproportionately affect certain groups. Low-income families feel the pain the most, and they have fewer options to deal with these challenges. Seniors on fixed incomes are also at risk, as they struggle to keep up with the increasing costs of living. For disabled individuals, affordability can be even harder to navigate, given the additional expenses that come with disability aids, medical care, and often limited access to affordable housing and transportation. The widening gap is making it harder for these groups to thrive, creating social tension and eroding trust in systems that should be providing a safety net.

But here's the thing: addressing the affordability crisis is not just a social issue; it's also a strategic necessity for Canada. With the possibility of a trade war with the US, Canada needs to ensure its economy is resilient and its people are economically secure. A strong domestic foundation is essential if we're going to weather the storm of any trade dispute. By tackling affordability, we not only improve the lives of Canadians but also fortify the economy. When people's basic needs are met, they spend more, they invest in local businesses, and they contribute to a healthy, growing economy. If people are struggling just to survive, they're less likely to spend money, and this can lead to broader economic stagnation. It's not just about people's day-to-day lives; it's about building a foundation for long-term economic success.

The affordability crisis is an issue that affects us all, but it also presents an opportunity. By addressing it head-on, Canada can strengthen its economy in ways that make it more adaptable and resilient to economic disruption, like a pandemic or trade war. When Canadians feel secure in their ability to afford housing, food, healthcare, and the essentials, they're more likely to contribute positively to the economy. Whether it's through their own spending or through increased worker productivity due to better health and housing security, the benefits are clear. Solving the affordability crisis isn't just a matter of fairness or social responsibility; it's a critical part of making sure Canada can hold its own in a changing global economy.

Neoliberalism

Neoliberalism has played a massive role in shaping the economic landscape in Canada, and not in a way that has benefited the majority of people. Over the years, we've seen a shift toward market-driven policies that prioritize profit over people. Tax cuts for the wealthy, deregulation, and a general preference for minimal government intervention have all contributed to a shrinking social safety net. This has made it harder for people who are already struggling to get the support they need. Instead of investing in programs that help people weather difficult times, like affordable healthcare or social assistance, the government has often chosen to lower taxes for the richest Canadians and large corporations. The idea is that if businesses are left to grow and prosper without much regulation, they will naturally create jobs and benefit everyone. But in practice, this hasn't happened.

What we've seen instead is that the gap between the rich and poor has grown wider. The wealthiest individuals and corporations have seen their wealth increase, while wages for working-class Canadians have stagnated. The promise of trickle-down economics, the idea that wealth would eventually reach the broader population, has been proven to be largely a myth. Meanwhile, essential services have been eroded. Health care, once a shining example of Canada's commitment to social welfare, has become strained under the pressure of privatization and cost-cutting measures. Many people have found themselves facing longer wait times and paying more out of pocket for services that were once covered. Social programs designed to provide a safety net for the most vulnerable have been cut or reduced, leaving people without the support they need during tough times.

This erosion of the safety net has had a ripple effect on inequality. As the middle class shrinks, more Canadians are falling into poverty, and the divide between the wealthy and the rest of society continues to grow. It's not just about money; it's about access to resources and opportunities. When the social safety net is strong, it gives people a chance to build a better life, even if they face setbacks. But when that net is weakened, it's harder for people to get ahead, and the barriers to success get higher. This creates an unstable society, where people feel disconnected from the larger social contract.

Canada needs to rethink its approach to neoliberal policies that have favoured the wealthy and the market over the well-being of its citizens. By rebuilding a strong social safety net, we can help ensure that people are protected from the economic pressures that have been exacerbated by neoliberal policies. This is especially important when looking ahead to a potential trade war with the US If Canada's people are economically secure, they can weather the storm of global trade tensions better than if they're already struggling. Investing in the affordability of life, through things like healthcare, housing, and income support, creates a resilient population that is less vulnerable to the external shocks of the global economy. Instead of prioritizing the wealth of a few, we need to focus on strengthening the economic position of everyone, so that when the economy faces challenges, we are all in a stronger place to respond.

Globalization has had a profound impact on the affordability crisis in Canada, and not necessarily in ways that benefit everyday people. The rise of outsourcing has played a key role in shifting good-paying jobs out of the country. For years, we've seen companies move manufacturing operations overseas, looking for cheaper labour and fewer regulations. As a result, many of the jobs that used to sustain working-class Canadians; jobs in manufacturing, textiles, and other industries disappeared. This contributed to wage stagnation, as fewer opportunities meant that workers had less bargaining power. What we've ended up with is a situation where the cost of living continues to rise, but the income levels for most people haven't kept pace. This widening affordability gap is one of the unfortunate side effects of an economy that prioritizes the bottom line over people's livelihoods.

At the same time, globalization has pushed housing markets into a state of hyperinflation. As investors from all around the world buy up real estate in major Canadian cities, the prices have skyrocketed. This isn't just an issue for people trying to buy a home, renting has become unaffordable as well. Local residents find themselves squeezed out by speculative investments from foreign buyers who have no intention of living in the properties they purchase. For many Canadians, the dream of homeownership is slipping further and further out of reach. The forces of globalization are making housing less of a commodity that serves the people and more of a speculative asset that serves the wealthy. This only deepens the affordability crisis, particularly for young people and families who are trying to secure stable housing in the midst of an increasingly competitive market.

The combination of wage stagnation and the rising costs of goods and services has left many Canadians struggling to keep up. Jobs that are left in Canada tend to be lower-paying, service-based positions, which do not provide the kind of financial security that a well-paying manufacturing or trade job once did. And because the cost of essentials like housing, food, and healthcare continues to climb, families are left with less and less disposable income. The benefits of globalization have certainly been felt by multinational corporations, but the average worker hasn't seen much of that trickle down.

As trade wars and economic tensions with the US continue to intensify, this becomes even more critical. If Canada is already feeling the squeeze of globalization, then a trade war with one of our largest trading partners will only worsen the situation. In this context, addressing the affordability crisis is not just a matter of social fairness; it's a matter of economic survival. Weathering the storm of a global economy that's becoming more volatile by the day is impossible if people are already struggling to make ends meet, with wages stuck in neutral and the cost of living steadily rising.

Shift In Government Spending

Over the past few decades, we've seen a shift in government spending priorities, one that has deepened economic inequality in Canada. Instead of investing in the welfare programs that support the most vulnerable in society, we've seen an increasing amount of government funds go into military spending and corporate tax cuts. These shifts are a direct result of neoliberal policies that prioritize national defence and corporate interests over the well-being of the average citizen. As a result, the social safety net has weakened, and the gap between the wealthy and the rest of the population has grown wider.

For years, welfare programs like unemployment insurance, social assistance, and public healthcare served as a safety net for people who were struggling to make ends meet. These programs helped ensure that, even when the economy faced downturns, people weren't left to fall through the cracks. But as governments have increasingly focused on military spending, the priorities have shifted. Instead of investing in programs that support working-class Canadians, the government has put more money into defence contracts and military equipment. While national security is important, the balance has tipped too far in one direction, and now we have a situation where the most vulnerable are often neglected in favour of spending on things that don't directly benefit the public.

Corporate tax cuts have followed a similar pattern. Large corporations, particularly multinational ones, have seen significant reductions in taxes, while at the same time, everyday Canadians are paying higher taxes to make up for the shortfall. The promise of these tax cuts was that corporations would invest in job creation and economic growth, but in many cases, those savings have simply gone into the pockets of executives and shareholders rather than being reinvested in the local economy. Instead of using the money to raise wages, create more jobs, or improve infrastructure, we've seen the rich get richer while the middle class shrinks. This has made the affordability crisis worse, as the government's fiscal policies have placed more strain on average Canadians who are already struggling to keep up with rising costs.

The unfortunate consequence of this shift in government spending is that it has made Canada more vulnerable to economic shocks, including the kind of trade war we could find ourselves in with the United States. If the government had been more focused on strengthening social safety nets and providing meaningful support to the public, Canadians would be in a better position to withstand external pressures. But with less investment in public health, affordable housing, and education, the country's ability to bounce back from a trade war is significantly weakened. People who are already living paycheck to paycheck, or struggling to afford basic necessities, won't have the resources they need to weather a trade war or an economic downturn.

What we've seen over the years is a system that rewards the wealthy and corporations while leaving the most vulnerable to fend for themselves. When the government shifts its spending away from welfare programs and toward military spending or corporate tax cuts, it exacerbates inequality and weakens the resilience of the economy. If we want to protect Canadians from the fallout of a trade war or any other economic turbulence, we need to rethink our priorities and shift the focus back toward policies that invest in the well-being of people.

Historical Failures In Housing Policy

When we look back at Canada's housing policies over the years, it's clear that we've fallen short in many ways. Affordable housing has been a persistent issue, and the lack of meaningful action on this front has made the affordability crisis even worse. One of the most glaring failures has been the rise of suburban sprawl, which has contributed to a huge disconnect between where people live and where they work. Rather than focusing on building affordable housing in the heart of cities or in places close to employment hubs, we've allowed suburban sprawl to take over. This has created long commutes, increased transportation costs, and disconnected communities. The focus has been on developing land cheaply and quickly, often without considering the long-term consequences.

Meanwhile, social housing has remained in short supply. There was a time when the Canadian government recognized the importance of social housing in addressing poverty and providing people with safe, affordable homes. But over the years, funding for social housing has been slashed, and we've seen a decline in the construction of public housing projects. Instead, the responsibility for housing was shifted to the private market, which has failed to deliver affordable homes for the majority of Canadians. As housing prices continue to rise, especially in urban centres, people are increasingly unable to afford decent places to live, and the gap between the wealthy and the rest of the population has only widened.

Part of the problem has been the focus on the private sector to handle the housing market. Developers and investors have had little incentive to build homes for low- and middle-income families. The priority has often been to build luxury condos or high-end properties that generate the most profit. As a result, we've seen a massive shortage of affordable rental units and homes for first-time buyers. Meanwhile, working-class Canadians are left to compete for the limited supply of affordable housing, pushing them further into the rental market or out of cities altogether.

This failure in housing policy has only made the affordability crisis more severe, especially as we consider the economic pressures of a trade war with the United States. If housing costs continue to rise, it's going to become even harder for Canadians to maintain financial stability, let alone weather the kind of economic turbulence that a trade war could bring. High housing costs put a strain on household budgets, leaving less room for savings, investments, or even the basics like food and healthcare. When people are struggling to pay for housing, they're less likely to have the financial resilience to cope with external shocks like tariffs or trade disruptions.

The lack of affordable housing is also contributing to inequality. Those who already own homes are seeing their property values soar, while renters and those trying to get on the property ladder are left behind. This deepens the wealth gap and makes it harder for people to improve their financial standing. If Canada had focused on building affordable housing and increasing the availability of social housing, we would be in a stronger position to handle economic disruption. Housing should be seen as a basic human right, not a commodity to be bought and sold for profit, and addressing this issue would go a long way in helping people weather the economic uncertainty that comes with global trade wars. Without a roof over their heads or a stable housing market, Canadians will be less equipped to face the financial pressures of a trade conflict with the US.

Rent Control And Housing Subsidies

Rent control and housing subsidies have been a topic of debate for years in Canada, with both supporters and critics offering their perspectives on their effectiveness. As housing costs continue to rise in major cities, these policies have been seen as essential tools for ensuring that people can still afford to live in urban centres without being pushed out by skyrocketing rents. Rent control policies, in particular, aim to keep rental prices stable and affordable for tenants, especially in markets where demand far outstrips supply. By limiting how much landlords can increase rents each year, these policies provide renters with some degree of financial predictability and protection against sudden price hikes.

The effectiveness of rent control, however, is not without its challenges. One issue is that it can discourage new construction or the maintenance of existing rental units. Developers and property owners may be less inclined to invest in new rental properties or make improvements to older ones if they feel their ability to charge market rents is limited. This can lead to a reduction in the overall quality of rental housing and fewer units available for people who need them. Additionally, rent control can create a situation where long-term tenants benefit, but newcomers or those looking to move may struggle to find affordable housing. When rent control is not implemented carefully, it can end up distorting the market and making it even harder for people to find suitable housing.

Housing subsidies, on the other hand, aim to assist individuals and families who are struggling to afford their rent or mortgage payments. These subsidies can come in the form of direct financial support or through programs that help people access affordable housing. Subsidies can make a significant difference in the lives of low- and middle-income families, allowing them to remain in their homes without having to sacrifice other essentials like food or healthcare. In Canada, programs like the National Housing Co-Investment Fund are designed to support the construction of affordable housing, while rent subsidies directly help individuals with the cost of living in high-demand areas.

While housing subsidies have shown to be beneficial, they also have their limitations. The main challenge is that subsidies often do not address the root cause of the problem: the lack of affordable housing supply. As long as demand for housing continues to outpace supply, subsidies will only provide temporary relief. There is a danger that relying too heavily on subsidies can delay the need for broader, more systemic changes in housing policy. Subsidies are a necessary short-term solution, but they don't fully address the long-term structural issues that drive up housing costs.

When it comes to navigating a potential trade war with the US, addressing the affordability crisis through policies like rent control and housing subsidies is important. In times of economic uncertainty, people need stability, and stable housing costs provide just that. If Canadians are burdened with high housing costs, they will have less disposable income to weather the shocks of tariffs, import restrictions, or other economic disruptions. Rent control and housing subsidies can help people hold on to their homes and avoid displacement, which strengthens the overall stability of communities. Moreover, by investing in affordable housing solutions, Canada can create a more resilient economy, one that is less vulnerable to economic disruption and more focused on the well-being of its citizens.

Public housing programs have long been an important tool for addressing housing affordability, especially in times of economic strain. When we look at how different countries, including Canada and various European nations, have approached the issue, it becomes clear that public housing can help alleviate housing stress and contribute to a more stable economy. In Canada, public housing has had periods of success, especially in the post-World War II era when large-scale development projects were undertaken to provide affordable housing for the growing population. Many cities saw the construction of well-planned communities that offered affordable rental options to families who might otherwise have struggled to find decent homes. These initiatives were particularly important for lower-income Canadians, who were often left out of the competitive housing market.

When we look at Europe, there are some standout examples of public housing models that have been particularly successful. In countries like the Netherlands, Denmark, and Sweden, public housing programs have been designed with a strong focus on sustainability, community integration, and long-term affordability. These countries tend to view housing as a fundamental human right, not just a commodity. They have adopted policies that allow for a robust public housing sector alongside the private market, which ensures that a range of housing options is available to people of all income levels. By investing in public housing, these countries have been able to stabilize housing markets, provide opportunities for social mobility, and prevent large portions of the population from being pushed into poverty due to housing costs.

Investing in public housing is also crucial for economic stability. When people have access to affordable housing, they are less likely to experience financial distress. Housing is one of the largest expenses for most families, so by reducing the burden of housing costs, public housing programs allow people to allocate their resources to other areas of the economy, such as education, healthcare, and transportation. This creates a more balanced and sustainable economic environment, where people are better able to contribute to the overall economy. Furthermore, when public housing is done well, it can become a catalyst for community development. It can provide stable housing in areas that have been economically depressed, which in turn can encourage local businesses to invest and thrive. The knock-on effects of such investments can benefit not just the individuals who receive housing support but also the broader community and economy.

When Canada is facing the challenges of a trade war, public housing programs can play a significant role in helping the country weather the storm. Economic instability caused by trade disruptions can lead to job losses, wage stagnation, and increased financial stress for many people. During these times, public housing programs can provide a buffer, ensuring that families are not displaced from their homes due to rising rents or job insecurity. Additionally, by ensuring that affordable housing remains available, Canada can maintain a more stable consumer base. People who are secure in their housing situation are more likely to continue spending on goods and services, helping to keep local businesses afloat and the economy moving forward.

In short, public housing programs, when implemented effectively, can serve as a pillar of economic stability. They not only address the immediate need for affordable housing but also contribute to the long-term health of the economy. By providing Canadians with access to stable housing, these programs reduce the financial stress that often leads to broader economic problems. In the face of a trade war, having a robust public housing sector can be an invaluable tool for ensuring that Canadian families and communities remain strong and resilient.

Zoning laws and urban planning policies play a huge role in shaping housing affordability. When you look at cities around the world, it's clear that restrictive zoning laws can contribute to a housing shortage by limiting where and how homes can be built. These laws often require developers to build larger, more expensive homes instead of allowing for more diverse types of housing options, like apartment buildings or smaller homes. This makes it harder for lower-income families or individuals to find affordable places to live, and it drives up the overall cost of housing in urban areas.

In places like Vancouver and Toronto, we've seen firsthand how restrictive zoning laws can create a housing crisis. These cities have had problems with housing affordability for years, and a big part of the issue is that their zoning laws have made it difficult to build the kind of affordable housing needed to meet the demand. In both cities, the availability of single-family homes in desirable neighbourhoods has been limited by zoning laws that keep new developments small and expensive. This leads to fewer homes being available for those who need them most, while driving up prices for everyone else. The result is an affordability crisis that makes it harder for many Canadians to find a place to live without spending an overwhelming portion of their income on rent or a mortgage.

However, there are cities that have started to make changes, showing how zoning reform can help ease the housing crisis. Take the example of Portland, Oregon, where city planners recognized that their zoning laws were contributing to high housing prices. The city decided to overhaul its zoning regulations to allow for more mixed-use developments, higher-density housing, and more affordable rental units. This reform helped increase the supply of affordable housing and made it easier for developers to build homes that are accessible to a wider range of income levels. By changing the rules around where and how buildings can be constructed, Portland created more opportunities for affordable housing to flourish, which in turn helped make housing more affordable for the average person.

Another example can be found in Minneapolis, Minnesota, which implemented a sweeping reform by eliminating single-family zoning across the city. This was a game-changer because it allowed for more multi-family homes, duplexes, and apartment buildings to be built in neighbourhoods that were previously restricted to single-family homes. The city recognized that the old zoning rules were contributing to segregation and limiting access to affordable housing for families and individuals who couldn't afford the rising cost of homeownership in those areas. By changing zoning laws to allow for more types of housing, Minneapolis made strides toward creating more equitable and affordable housing options, helping to reduce the housing gap and making it easier for people of all incomes to find a place to live.

These examples show that urban planning and zoning reform can be effective tools for addressing the affordability crisis. By loosening zoning restrictions, cities can encourage the development of a more diverse range of housing options, which helps meet the needs of all residents. If Canadian cities were to adopt similar reforms, we could see a decrease in the pressure on the housing market, making it easier for people to find affordable homes. This is particularly important in the face of a trade war with the US, where economic uncertainty could lead to more job losses and greater financial strain on families. If housing remains affordable during tough times, Canadians are more likely to be able to weather the storm and maintain their quality of life. Reforming zoning laws could be a key step in ensuring that Canadians can access affordable housing and, in turn, help stabilize the economy as a whole.

The Changing Food Landscape

Food prices have been steadily rising, and they're growing faster than wages in many cases. This is a huge problem for people already struggling to make ends meet. When food becomes more expensive, it takes up a larger portion of household budgets, which means there's less money available for other essential things like rent or healthcare. If wages aren't keeping up with food prices, low-income families are hit the hardest. They're the ones who already have limited resources, so when costs climb, their situation only gets worse.

In Canada, the cost of food has jumped dramatically in recent years, particularly for basics like vegetables, dairy, and meat. For example, the price of fresh fruit and vegetables has been rising at rates far outpacing the rate of inflation. These price hikes make it even harder for families to maintain a healthy diet, as healthier options tend to be the most expensive. The result is that many families are forced to choose between paying for food and paying for other necessities. For some, that means relying on less nutritious, cheaper food options that aren't good for long-term health.

Food insecurity is a growing issue, especially for those already living paycheck to paycheck. It's hard to get by when food costs are out of reach, and it's even harder when people live in food deserts. These are areas where grocery stores are few and far between, and where affordable, healthy food is hard to find. Instead of supermarkets, people in food deserts often have to rely on convenience stores or fast food chains, where the options are limited and overpriced. For families living in these areas, the cost of food can be even more significant because of the lack of competition and choice. They may be paying more for less, and the impact on their health and well-being can be long-lasting.

Food banks have become a lifeline for many families in Canada, but they're not a sustainable solution. More people than ever are turning to food banks to get the basics, and the number of people relying on them has increased steadily. According to reports from Food Banks Canada, millions of people used food banks in recent years, and a significant portion of those people are children. The fact that food banks are becoming more and more necessary shows just how dire the situation has become. They are a stopgap measure, but they don't address the underlying problem of rising food prices and wages that aren't increasing at the same rate.

The affordability crisis, especially in food, is not just a matter of individual hardship; it's a broader issue that impacts communities and the economy as a whole. When people can't afford to feed their families, it leads to greater health problems, more financial strain, and a less productive society overall. The challenge of food insecurity is one of many factors that contribute to the affordability crisis in Canada. But if we can tackle it head-on by addressing the root causes, like rising food prices and low wages, we can start to make progress. Doing so would also help stabilize the economy as a whole and make Canada more resilient, especially if we end up facing a trade war with the US. A healthy population that's well-fed and secure in their ability to access food is a key piece of a stable, thriving society, and addressing food insecurity is a critical step in building that future.

Subsidies And Public Support Programs

Government programs like food stamps and school meal programs play a crucial role in alleviating hunger, particularly for low-income families. These types of support help ensure that people don't have to choose between paying for food and paying for other essentials. In a country like Canada, where rising food prices are outpacing wages, these subsidies and public support programs become even more important. They provide a safety net that makes sure no one has to go without food simply because they don't have the financial means. When people can rely on these programs, they are more likely to stay healthy, work more effectively, and contribute to the economy without the constant stress of worrying about where their next meal will come from.

Programs like food stamps, or the Canadian equivalent, which could be thought of as a version of income support for food, provide people with the means to buy groceries. For families already living on tight budgets, this type of assistance can make a world of difference. It helps level the playing field, ensuring that even the most vulnerable individuals can afford healthy food. Without these programs, many families would face extreme hardship and possibly turn to food banks or other emergency services, which, while helpful, are not sustainable long-term solutions.

School meal programs also play a vital role in ensuring children don't go hungry, especially when parents are struggling to make ends meet. These programs help children get the nutrition they need during the school day, which is important for their growth, learning, and overall well-being. When children aren't worried about whether they will have lunch at school, they can focus more on their studies, participate in activities, and be more engaged in the educational process. This not only helps children in the short term but also sets them up for better success in the future. If children are getting enough to eat and are in a stable environment, they're more likely to perform well in school and have better life outcomes, which in turn can contribute positively to the overall economy in the long run.

These programs also make economic sense. By providing subsidies and support, the government ensures that people can maintain some level of dignity and independence, preventing extreme poverty and the social instability that can come with it. Additionally, helping families meet their basic needs means that they can continue to participate in the economy, whether by purchasing goods, paying for services, or engaging in the workforce. If people are going hungry, it limits their ability to contribute fully to society, and that in turn impacts economic productivity.

In a broader context, subsidies and public support programs like food stamps and school meal programs can help Canada weather any economic storms, including a trade war with the US. These programs help make sure that even if the economy takes a hit, people won't fall through the cracks. They ensure that families have the stability they need to get through tough times without the added burden of food insecurity. When the government steps in with these kinds of support programs, it strengthens the country's resilience, not just in times of peace, but in times of trade conflict or other economic challenges as well.

Local Food Movements And Sustainability

Local food movements, community gardens, and food cooperatives are playing a crucial role in making food more affordable and accessible, particularly for communities that are struggling with rising prices. These grassroots initiatives not only provide healthy, fresh food but also help reduce dependency on large corporate food chains, which are often responsible for driving up food prices through their control over the market. By focusing on local food systems, communities can ensure that the food they eat is grown and produced in their own neighbourhoods, reducing transportation costs and cutting down on the carbon footprint of food production.

Community gardens are a prime example of how local food movements work. In many urban areas, vacant lots are transformed into thriving gardens that provide fresh produce to local residents. These gardens help to address food insecurity by giving people direct access to affordable, nutritious food. Community members often come together to plant, grow, and harvest the food, which creates a sense of community and strengthens local bonds. People are not only able to feed their families with the fruits and vegetables they grow, but they also learn valuable skills related to gardening and food production. These community-based initiatives help take pressure off the broader food system, where costs continue to rise due to the dominance of large food corporations.

Food cooperatives are another example of how local food movements are making a difference. These co-ops operate on a model where community members have a direct stake in the business, which means that the focus is on providing affordable food rather than maximizing profits. In a food cooperative, the prices are typically lower than in large corporate grocery stores, and the food is often sourced from local farmers and producers. This helps keep money within the community and reduces the reliance on big corporations that are often disconnected from the areas they serve. Co-ops often prioritize sustainability as well, sourcing food that is grown or produced using environmentally friendly practices, which benefits both the local economy and the planet.

Supporting these local food initiatives can help Canada become more self-sufficient in terms of food production. Instead of relying on imported goods or corporate-controlled food systems, communities can create their own sustainable sources of food. This not only makes food more affordable but also provides healthier options to people who might not otherwise have access to fresh produce. When local food systems thrive, it helps create a more resilient food supply chain that is less vulnerable to external shocks, such as the fluctuations in prices caused by trade wars or other global disruptions.

In the context of a trade war with the US, local food movements and sustainable food systems can help Canada protect itself from external economic pressures. By focusing on local production and consumption, Canada can reduce its reliance on imports from other countries, including the US. This creates a more stable food system that is less susceptible to price hikes or supply shortages that might arise from trade disputes. By investing in local food movements and community-based solutions, Canada can build a more resilient economy and create a food system that is not only more affordable but also more sustainable in the long run.

The High Cost Of Privatization

The high cost of privatization, especially in healthcare, is a pressing issue that deeply impacts affordability, particularly for low-income and marginalized groups. When healthcare systems are privatized, it shifts the burden from the state to individuals, meaning that people have to rely on private insurance companies to cover their medical costs. In places like the US, where privatized healthcare is the norm, this system results in astronomical costs for individuals, with many forced to choose between paying for medical care and covering basic needs like housing or food. The affordability gap is made worse by the fact that low-income people often can't afford the premiums, deductibles, and co-pays that come with private insurance. Even if they have insurance, many face significant out-of-pocket expenses when it comes to treatments, prescriptions, or emergency care.

This gap is even wider for marginalized groups, including racial minorities, people living with disabilities, and those in rural or low-income areas. These groups often face systemic barriers that limit their access to quality healthcare. In the US, the privatized system exacerbates these issues, as insurance companies have little incentive to prioritize health outcomes over profits. People without access to employer-sponsored insurance or who are uninsured often rely on emergency rooms or public health programs, which may be overburdened or underfunded. The lack of universal healthcare means that those who cannot afford insurance have to navigate an unpredictable system where the cost of care is continually rising, without guarantees of adequate coverage.

When healthcare becomes a commodity rather than a public service, the result is an inequality in access. Wealthier individuals can afford the best care available, while those at the bottom of the income ladder often have no choice but to accept subpar services or go without treatment altogether. This not only affects individuals' health but also leads to a greater strain on the economy as a whole. People who cannot afford care may end up in worse health, unable to work, or reliant on emergency services, creating additional costs for the public system to pick up. When healthcare is treated as a business, the system becomes one where only those with means can access necessary services, while everyone else struggles to keep up.

In contrast, Canada's healthcare system, which is publicly funded and provides coverage to all citizens regardless of income, addresses some of these problems by removing the financial barriers to care. While Canada's system isn't perfect, the difference is striking when compared to the privatized systems in the US The fact that healthcare is seen as a public good rather than a commodity means that everyone has access to the care they need, not just those who can afford it. This helps bridge the affordability gap, particularly for vulnerable populations who otherwise would not be able to afford insurance or pay high medical costs.

As trade conflicts impact the cost of living and push more people into financial hardship, having a robust, publicly funded healthcare system ensures that people don't have to face an additional burden. If Canada were to shift towards privatized healthcare or allow more private insurance schemes to take hold, it could widen the affordability gap and create even more pressure on low-income families. As healthcare costs rise in a privatized system, Canada could find itself in a similar situation to the US, with healthcare becoming a luxury that only the wealthy can afford. This would not only hurt the most vulnerable in society but would also leave Canada more exposed to economic disruption, particularly in the face of external challenges like a trade war. The key to maintaining stability in such times is ensuring that basic needs, including healthcare, remain affordable and accessible to all.

Mental Health And Dental Coverage

Mental health and dental care are often overlooked when discussing healthcare systems, yet they play a critical role in both individual well-being and the broader economy. The importance of having access to comprehensive healthcare, which includes mental health services and dental care, cannot be overstated. Mental health issues, like depression, anxiety, and stress, are among the leading causes of disability worldwide. These conditions not only impact people's day-to-day lives but also have long-term effects on their ability to work, interact socially, and take care of their families. When mental health care is not included in the public healthcare system, people who cannot afford private treatment are left to suffer in silence or rely on underfunded public programs. This creates a cycle where mental health issues remain untreated, worsening over time and leading to greater long-term costs both for the individual and the economy.

Dental care is similarly crucial for maintaining overall health. Poor oral health can lead to a range of other health problems, from heart disease to diabetes, and untreated dental issues can escalate into severe conditions that require expensive emergency treatments. However, in many countries, including the US, dental care is separated from general healthcare and is often only available through private insurance or paid out-of-pocket. This creates a significant barrier for low-income individuals, who may not be able to afford regular check-ups or the cost of necessary dental procedures. In Canada, the inclusion of dental care in the public healthcare system would alleviate some of these barriers, ensuring that individuals have access to the care they need before problems escalate into more serious and expensive conditions.

When mental health and dental care are included in a universal public healthcare system, the long-term benefits are substantial. People are more likely to seek treatment early, preventing minor issues from developing into major, costly problems. For example, a person with depression is more likely to take steps to manage their condition if mental health services are readily available. Similarly, someone experiencing dental pain is more likely to visit a dentist regularly if the cost is not a barrier. This early intervention reduces the need for expensive treatments down the road and leads to healthier individuals who are better able to contribute to the economy. Healthy individuals are more productive, miss fewer days of work, and are less likely to require long-term disability support.

In the context of a trade war with the US, the importance of comprehensive healthcare becomes even more apparent. If Canada were to face a trade conflict that disrupts the economy, the last thing the country needs is to have more people falling through the cracks because they cannot access mental health or dental care. A robust public healthcare system that includes these services ensures that people are taken care of, regardless of their income level. This means fewer people are out of work due to untreated health conditions, and fewer people are relying on expensive emergency care because they couldn't afford preventive treatment. In turn, this helps stabilize the economy by reducing the financial strain on public resources, allowing the country to better withstand external economic shocks.

Including mental health and dental care in public healthcare is not just about treating individuals; it is about creating a healthier, more stable society. When people can take care of their mental and physical health, they are more likely to lead productive, fulfilling lives. This improves overall well-being, reduces societal inequality, and helps foster a more resilient economy. If Canada can ensure these services are available to all, it will be better positioned to weather challenges like a trade war, supporting its population and economy in the process.

Healthcare costs are one of the biggest financial burdens on individuals and governments alike. As these costs continue to rise, the need for effective cost control mechanisms becomes more urgent. One of the most effective ways to keep healthcare costs down is through drug price negotiations and bulk purchasing. These approaches have been proven to work in countries like Canada, where the government negotiates the prices of medications on behalf of the public. By doing this, the government ensures that it gets the best possible price for the drugs it purchases, ultimately reducing the financial burden on patients. This is an area where Canada has been able to keep costs relatively under control compared to the US, where drug prices are often far higher, and the lack of negotiation creates an environment where companies can charge whatever they want.

Bulk purchasing is another tool that can significantly lower healthcare costs. In many countries, bulk purchasing programs are used to buy medications and medical supplies in large quantities, which reduces the per-unit price. This is especially beneficial in countries like Canada, where the healthcare system is publicly funded. Bulk purchasing ensures that the government can buy the medications and supplies needed for the population at a fraction of the cost that individual consumers or private insurance companies would pay. It also creates a more efficient system, as large-scale purchases reduce the administrative costs associated with managing multiple small transactions. The same principles of cost control can be applied to other sectors of the economy, including housing and education, where bulk purchasing or negotiated pricing could make essential goods and services more affordable for everyone.

The key to incorporating these mechanisms into other systems for better affordability is finding ways to increase the negotiating power of the public sector. In housing, for example, governments could use their collective purchasing power to negotiate lower construction costs for affordable housing projects. This could be achieved by negotiating with contractors and suppliers to get better prices on materials, labor, and equipment, similar to how drug prices are negotiated. This would make it more affordable for the government to build new affordable housing units, reducing the cost to taxpayers and increasing the availability of homes for low-income individuals and families.

Similarly, in education, governments could negotiate with educational institutions to reduce the cost of tuition or the price of textbooks. By using collective bargaining power, governments could push for lower prices on essential educational resources, making education more accessible to everyone, especially those from disadvantaged backgrounds. These cost control mechanisms would not only help reduce the financial burden on individuals but also improve overall access to essential services like healthcare, housing, and education.

Cost control mechanisms like drug price negotiations and bulk purchasing can help Canada protect its economy and ensure that the public continues to have access to essential services, even during times of economic instability. By keeping healthcare costs down and making other essential services more affordable, the government can reduce the strain on individuals and families, preventing the affordability crisis from becoming even more severe. The government's ability to negotiate on behalf of the public ensures that Canada can continue to provide high-quality services without sacrificing its economic stability. This helps the country weather external challenges, such as a trade war, by creating a more resilient system that is less vulnerable to rising costs and external pressures.

The Essential Nature Of Utilities

Utilities are one of the most basic necessities in any modern society. Access to water, electricity, and the internet is not just a convenience but something that we rely on every single day. Yet, for many households, the rising costs of these utilities are becoming an increasingly heavy burden, especially for lower-income families. Water, electricity, and heating are all essential for everything from keeping our homes livable to accessing education, healthcare, and even jobs. The fact that these utilities are becoming more expensive has a ripple effect that goes far beyond just higher monthly bills.

Water is something we all need, and when the cost of it rises, it hits people who are already struggling the hardest. For families living paycheck to paycheck, every added expense makes life that much harder. If you are barely scraping by, the thought of paying for something that should be a basic human right becomes overwhelming. The same can be said for electricity. It's not just about turning on the lights. It's about keeping your home warm in the winter or cool in the summer, cooking your food, and even just charging your phone. For lower-income families, these rising costs can make it difficult to keep up, forcing some to make hard choices between paying for essentials like food or covering their utility bills. No one should have to make that kind of choice.

The affordability crisis we're facing right now doesn't just stop with food and housing. Utilities are just as much a part of the equation, and if we don't address these rising costs, we're only going to see the gap between the haves and the have-nots widen even more. We need to recognize that utilities are not luxuries; they are basic services that every person should have access to at an affordable rate. When costs continue to climb, lower-income households are the first to feel the strain, and it only adds to the burden they are already carrying.

If we want to ensure that everyone has access to the basics they need to thrive, we have to address the affordability of utilities. This is especially crucial when we consider how a trade war with the US could impact Canada. In times of economic instability, the cost of living tends to rise, and this is when the most vulnerable are hit hardest. By making sure that essential utilities are kept affordable, we help shield low-income households from the worst effects of economic stress. This means that even in the midst of a trade war or economic downturn, Canadians can still rely on the basics to live their lives without falling into deeper poverty. Ensuring access to affordable utilities is an important step toward maintaining social stability and economic resilience, particularly when external pressures threaten to make life even harder for those already struggling.

Public Versus Private Utilities

When it comes to utilities, one of the most fundamental choices we face is whether they should be publicly or privately run. It's a big question because the way we manage utilities like water, electricity, and gas directly impacts the affordability of those services. Publicly run utilities have a long history of providing stable, affordable services to people. These utilities are owned by the government and funded by taxpayer dollars, so their main goal isn't to generate profits for shareholders. Instead, the focus is on providing essential services to the public at a price people can afford. This often leads to more stability in pricing and ensures that everyone has access to the basics they need.

Privatized utilities, on the other hand, are run by private companies that are primarily focused on making money. While they can be efficient and innovative, their main goal is to maximize profits. This often leads to price hikes as companies work to keep their shareholders happy. Unlike publicly run utilities, privatized ones don't have the same kind of built-in safeguards to prevent price gouging, which means the cost of basic services can rise much faster than wages. The result is that people, especially those in lower-income brackets, are forced to pay more for services they can't live without. And when prices go up, it's not just a matter of people paying more out of pocket; it often means they have to make sacrifices elsewhere, like cutting back on food or healthcare.

Research has shown that public utilities are more effective at keeping prices stable. For example, a study comparing electricity prices in countries with publicly run utilities versus those with privatized systems found that countries with public utilities often have lower rates and more predictable pricing. This is partly because public utilities are able to focus on long-term goals instead of short-term profits. They also tend to have more accountability because they're directly controlled by the government, which means there are more checks and balances in place to prevent price manipulation or price hikes without justification. In contrast, privatized utilities are more likely to raise prices quickly in response to market changes, without the same level of oversight.

Publicly run utilities also tend to be more accessible to a wider range of people. Since the goal isn't to maximize profit, these services are typically available to everyone, regardless of income level. Privatized utilities, on the other hand, often operate in areas where they can make the most money, which means that low-income or rural areas might be left with fewer options or higher prices. This is especially concerning when we think about people who are already struggling to make ends meet. If their utility prices are going up because of privatization, it's just another added cost they can't afford.

When we look at the overall impact, public utilities have a clear advantage when it comes to keeping prices stable and affordable. They help ensure that everyone, regardless of their income or where they live, has access to the essential services they need. This is particularly important when we're considering how to navigate a potential trade war with the US if Canada is going to stand strong in the face of external economic pressures, ensuring that the basics, like utilities, remain affordable for everyone is crucial. Publicly run utilities can be a key part of that strategy, providing Canadians with the stability and reliability they need to weather difficult times.

When we look at the affordability of basic services like utilities, one of the most effective ways governments can step in is through subsidies and price controls. These policies can directly ease the financial burden on households, particularly those that are struggling to keep up with rising costs. Subsidies are essentially financial aids that governments provide to reduce the price people have to pay for essential services like electricity, water, or gas. Price controls, on the other hand, set limits on how high companies can charge for these services. Both of these tools can play a significant role in ensuring that families aren't forced to choose between paying their utility bills and other necessities like food or healthcare.

Subsidies are particularly important for lower-income households. In many places, basic services can take up a huge chunk of a family's monthly budget. By offering subsidies, the government can help make sure that these essential services are more affordable. For example, in some parts of Canada, energy subsidies are offered to households that fall below a certain income threshold. These subsidies can reduce electricity bills, allowing families to use more energy without worrying about it draining their finances. The impact of this can be huge, especially in colder climates where heating costs are a significant portion of household expenses. Without subsidies, many people would be left to either face high bills they can't afford or go without heating and other critical services.

Price controls are another tool governments use to ensure that essential services remain affordable. In some regions, price controls have been used on water and electricity to prevent large price hikes from overwhelming consumers. When utilities are privatized or when market forces are left unchecked, prices can skyrocket. But price controls help prevent that by setting a cap on how much a company can charge. These controls are especially helpful in areas where there is little competition, as they prevent monopolies from charging whatever they want. By keeping prices within reasonable limits, governments can ensure that people aren't overburdened by the cost of these services.

There are plenty of examples around the world where subsidies and price controls have worked well. One good case study is in some European countries, where governments have successfully used subsidies to keep energy prices low for vulnerable populations. In Germany, for example, low-income families benefit from energy subsidies that help them pay their heating bills during the cold months. These subsidies ensure that even the most financially stressed households can keep their homes warm without sacrificing other basic needs. In places like France, price controls have been used on electricity rates to keep them from rising too fast. These policies have helped reduce the impact of rising energy costs, and the success stories show that it is possible to keep utility prices under control when there is a political will to do so.

The success of these policies in Europe shows that with the right approach, governments can use subsidies and price controls to make sure that people's basic needs are met without breaking the bank. For Canada, this could be a game changer in dealing with the affordability crisis, especially when navigating economic pressures from a trade war with the US If the government were to expand its use of subsidies and price controls on essential services, it could help shield Canadians from the worst effects of inflation and market fluctuations. This approach doesn't just help in the short term; it helps build a more resilient economy that can withstand external shocks, like trade wars, by keeping household spending in check and ensuring that people don't fall into deeper poverty.

Green Energy And Sustainable Practices

One of the most important steps we can take to address the affordability crisis is to make the transition to renewable energy sources. Green energy isn't just a way to reduce our environmental footprint; it's also an investment in long-term savings. By focusing on sustainable energy, like wind, solar, and hydroelectric power, Canada can significantly reduce the cost of utilities for households. The initial investment in renewable energy infrastructure may seem high, but once the systems are in place, the long-term savings are substantial. The shift to green energy is not just about reducing carbon emissions; it's also about ensuring that future generations are not burdened by rising energy costs due to our dependence on fossil fuels.

One of the key benefits of renewable energy is its ability to lower the volatility of energy prices. Traditional energy sources like oil and gas are subject to the whims of global markets. If a country like the US or Saudi Arabia faces disruptions in production or if trade tensions escalate, energy prices can spike, leading to higher utility bills. But renewable energy, once established, offers a more stable cost structure. Solar and wind power, for example, rely on natural resources that are essentially free, sunlight and wind, and as the technology to harness them continues to improve, the cost of generating power from these sources will continue to decrease. This makes energy bills much more predictable and less subject to market fluctuations, which helps households plan and budget without fear of sudden price hikes.

In places where renewable energy policies have been properly implemented, the benefits are clear. Take Denmark, for example. Denmark has invested heavily in wind energy, and as a result, it now produces a significant portion of its electricity from wind turbines. This investment has not only helped reduce the country's carbon footprint but has also led to a reduction in electricity costs over time. The government's commitment to green energy has made the country less reliant on expensive fossil fuels, which means citizens don't face the same kind of unpredictable energy price hikes seen in other parts of the world. It also makes the country more energy-independent, which in turn reduces the impact of external pressures, like trade wars or conflicts that might affect oil supplies.

Canada, with its vast natural resources, is uniquely positioned to lead the way in renewable energy. The country already has some success stories, especially in hydroelectric power, which accounts for a significant portion of Canada's energy generation. Expanding these kinds of green energy sources, alongside the development of solar and wind energy, could make Canada even less reliant on imported energy and fossil fuels. This would not only lower energy costs but also improve energy security in the long term. Imagine a future where Canadian homes rely on clean, renewable energy, and their electricity bills are predictable and affordable. That's a future where families can focus on other aspects of life without constantly worrying about whether they can afford their next power bill.

The importance of green energy is not just about the environment or the economy; it's about providing stability and security to Canadians in an uncertain world. The rising costs of traditional energy sources are a major part of the affordability crisis. By committing to renewable energy, Canada can reduce the financial burden on households, making energy more affordable and stable. It's not a short-term fix but rather a long-term solution that can help us weather economic storms, like a trade war with the US, by reducing our reliance on foreign energy markets and fossil fuels. In the end, a stronger, more sustainable energy system is a crucial part of building a resilient economy and ensuring that Canadians can thrive, no matter what challenges lie ahead.

The Growing Costs Of Transportation

Transportation costs have become a major source of financial strain for many Canadian families. Over the years, fuel prices have steadily climbed, and car maintenance has become increasingly expensive. For families who rely on personal vehicles to get to work, school, or other essential activities, these rising costs have made it harder to make ends meet. It's not just the price of fuel that adds up; the ongoing costs of maintaining a car—things like insurance, repairs, and registration—can be overwhelming, especially for those already living paycheck to paycheck. As the cost of transportation rises, it eats into the money families have left for other basic needs, like food, housing, and healthcare.

In addition to the higher costs of owning and maintaining a car, traffic congestion in many cities has made commuting even more expensive. Longer commute times mean more fuel consumption, which not only affects the environment but also further strains household budgets. In some parts of Canada, the cost of commuting has become so high that families are considering alternative options like public transportation or carpooling. However, for many, public transit options are limited or inadequate, particularly in smaller cities or rural areas. For these families, owning and maintaining a car is often seen as the only viable option, despite the financial burden it creates.

The rise in transportation costs can also be linked to the broader affordability crisis. When people have to spend more on getting from place to place, they have less disposable income for other important areas of life. The burden of high fuel prices, car repairs, and insurance premiums falls disproportionately on lower-income families who have fewer resources to absorb these costs. As transportation becomes more expensive, it limits mobility and access to better opportunities for these families. It's harder to get to work, harder to access education or healthcare, and harder to participate in the economy when the cost of simply getting around is so high.

Rising transportation costs also have a ripple effect on the cost of goods and services. When it becomes more expensive for businesses to transport goods across the country, those higher costs are passed on to consumers. This contributes to inflation and makes everything from groceries to household products more expensive. For families already struggling with basic expenses, the added burden of rising transportation costs only makes the affordability crisis worse. Addressing these rising transportation costs is a critical piece of the puzzle when it comes to ensuring that Canadians can continue to thrive in an environment of growing economic uncertainty.

One way to tackle these challenges is by investing in more affordable and efficient public transportation systems. By reducing reliance on personal vehicles, we can alleviate some of the pressure on families who are struggling to pay for their daily commutes. Expanding and improving public transportation would not only lower transportation costs for individuals but also reduce overall congestion, which can improve the quality of life for everyone. At the same time, policies aimed at reducing fuel costs or supporting cleaner, more efficient transportation options could help lessen the impact of rising transportation costs on Canadian households. These solutions could make it easier for people to get around without facing financial hardship, contributing to a more affordable and equitable society.

As Canada navigates economic challenges, including the potential for a trade war with the US, addressing the growing costs of transportation can help ensure that the affordability crisis does not worsen. By focusing on policies that reduce transportation expenses and increase access to more affordable transportation options, Canada can build a stronger, more resilient economy that benefits everyone, not just those at the top. Reducing the financial strain of getting from place to place would help families keep more of their hard-earned money, allowing them to invest in other aspects of their lives and contributing to the long-term stability of the Canadian economy.

Public Transportation Investment

Public transportation systems have long been one of the most effective ways to reduce transportation costs and make cities more accessible for people at all income levels. Looking at successful examples from cities like Toronto, Vancouver, and various European cities can provide some valuable insights into how investments in public transit can ease the financial burden on individuals while also benefiting the broader economy.

In Toronto, for instance, the city's extensive subway and bus networks have played a crucial role in reducing the reliance on personal vehicles. With millions of people relying on the public transportation system every day, it's clear that investment in such infrastructure makes a real difference. The Toronto Transit Commission (TTC) offers a variety of options, from buses to streetcars, which serve different parts of the city, making it easier for people to get to work, school, or other essential places without the need for a car. As a result, many families, particularly those with lower incomes, can avoid the high costs of car ownership, including fuel, insurance, and maintenance. The cost of transportation becomes more predictable and manageable, allowing people to allocate their finances to other areas of life.

Vancouver has also made significant strides in improving its public transportation system, particularly with the SkyTrain, a driverless rapid transit system that connects the city to its suburbs. The SkyTrain, along with buses and ferries, has helped reduce traffic congestion and lower transportation costs for residents. The affordability of public transit in Vancouver has helped make the city more livable, especially for those who do not own cars. In fact, Vancouver's approach has been praised for its focus on sustainability and environmental benefits, as the city has worked to reduce its carbon footprint by investing in clean, efficient transportation systems. These kinds of policies not only benefit the people who use them directly but also help make the overall transportation system more efficient, reducing the strain on infrastructure and the environment.

When looking at European cities like Copenhagen, Zurich, and Amsterdam, the focus on robust and affordable public transportation is even more evident. These cities have long prioritized cycling, walking, and efficient public transit to create more sustainable urban environments. In Copenhagen, for example, a combination of buses, trains, and bike lanes has drastically reduced the city's reliance on cars. The Danish capital has one of the highest rates of cycling in the world, and its efficient public transit system makes it easy for people to get around without needing to own a car. This has not only lowered transportation costs for individuals but also helped reduce traffic congestion and pollution, creating a cleaner, healthier city for everyone.

The key takeaway from these successful case studies is that investing in public transportation is one of the most effective ways to address the rising costs of commuting and make cities more accessible to people from all walks of life. When people have access to affordable and efficient transportation options, they are less reliant on private vehicles, which can be a significant financial burden. Public transit not only provides a more affordable option for individuals but also contributes to less congested, more sustainable urban environments. These systems also improve access to essential services, such as healthcare and education, making it easier for people to participate fully in the economy and society.

In the context of a potential trade war with the US, addressing the affordability of transportation could be a powerful tool for Canada to strengthen its resilience. By reducing transportation costs through investment in public transit, Canada can alleviate some of the pressure on households that might otherwise be hit hard by economic instability. Additionally, a more efficient public transit system could help improve productivity by reducing the time people spend in traffic and ensuring they can get to work and other essential locations without unnecessary delays. Investing in public transportation is not just about providing a service; it's about strengthening the overall economy and improving the quality of life for Canadians, especially those who are most vulnerable to rising costs.

Rural Transportation Challenges

Rural communities in Canada face a unique set of challenges when it comes to transportation. Unlike urban centers where public transit systems can offer affordable and efficient options, rural areas are often left with limited or no access to such services. This creates a significant barrier to mobility for people living outside of major cities, particularly those in lower-income brackets. For many rural Canadians, owning a car becomes a necessity rather than a choice. Unfortunately, with rising fuel prices, maintenance costs, and the burden of vehicle ownership, this option quickly becomes unaffordable for some. The lack of affordable transportation not only impacts the ability to get to work or school but also limits access to healthcare, grocery stores, and other essential services.

One of the most pressing issues for rural communities is the sheer distance between residents and the resources they need. In small towns and villages, public transportation options are often nonexistent or so limited that they are unreliable for everyday use. A person in a rural area may have to travel long distances to see a doctor or attend a job interview, which can be a major challenge when public transit doesn't run frequently or at all. For people who can't afford to own a car, this can be a serious problem. Rural transportation needs to be more than just a way to get from point A to point B; it needs to be a service that connects people to opportunities and services that allow them to live healthy, productive lives.

There are a few possible solutions to help bridge the gap in rural transportation. One option that's gaining traction is shared car programs. These programs allow people to share vehicles with others in their community, making it easier to get around without the burden of full car ownership. In some areas, car-sharing programs have been set up to allow people to book cars when needed, without having to pay for maintenance, insurance, or other costs associated with owning a car.

This reduces the financial barrier to transportation and makes it easier for people who only need a vehicle occasionally to access one when necessary.

Regional transit systems are another potential solution for rural areas. These systems would provide scheduled bus routes or shuttle services between rural communities and larger towns or cities. The idea is to create a more organized and reliable transportation network that links rural residents to larger centers where they can access services, education, and employment. These transit systems could also be adjusted to fit the specific needs of rural areas, such as providing transportation for seniors or people with disabilities. By pooling resources and working with municipalities or provincial governments, regional transit could make it easier and more affordable for people in rural areas to get around.

While these solutions aren't perfect and may not work for every rural area, they represent an opportunity to start addressing some of the transportation issues that rural communities face. The affordability crisis in Canada is only worsened by the lack of access to reliable transportation, especially for those living in rural areas. If the government can invest in solutions like shared car programs and regional transit, it could significantly reduce transportation costs for rural Canadians and improve their access to essential services. In the context of a trade war with the US, these kinds of investments in rural transportation could help ensure that people in every part of Canada are equipped to handle the challenges ahead. It's not just about getting from place to place; it's about making sure that everyone, regardless of where they live, has the tools and opportunities they need to thrive in a changing world.

Making Insurance Affordable

Affordable insurance plays a critical role in providing a safety net for households, especially those with lower incomes. Health, life, and disability insurance are key protections that help individuals and families manage the unpredictable events that life throws their way. Without access to affordable insurance, many people find themselves exposed to financial hardship when faced with illness, injury, or even death. Health insurance is the most immediate concern for many. Without it, medical bills can quickly spiral out of control, especially for those who already have limited financial resources. The rising cost of healthcare in Canada, even with its public system, means that many low-income individuals and families struggle to afford prescriptions, dental care, or mental health services, which are often not covered by provincial insurance. If people can't afford these necessary services, their health will suffer, and over time, their ability to work and contribute to the economy will diminish.

Life insurance is another area where affordability is crucial. For low-income households, life insurance can provide a sense of security that their family will not be left in financial ruin if the worst happens. It can cover funeral expenses, help pay off debts, and ensure that children have access to basic needs even in the absence of a breadwinner. The reality is that many working-class families live paycheck to paycheck and do not have the luxury of setting aside significant savings for a rainy day, let alone for an emergency like a death in the family. Without life insurance, these families are at risk of slipping further into poverty.

Disability insurance serves a similar purpose but for a different kind of threat. If someone becomes too ill or injured to work, they can quickly find themselves in a dire situation, especially if they do not have adequate financial support. Low-income workers are especially vulnerable in this area because they often lack the savings or resources to weather the storm of a sudden disability. Disability insurance can replace a portion of lost income, which is a lifeline for many people who would otherwise have no way to support themselves or their families. However, the cost of disability insurance is often too high for people living paycheck to paycheck, leaving them vulnerable to financial ruin if an unexpected medical issue arises.

The importance of making insurance more affordable cannot be overstated, especially for low-income households that are already dealing with the strain of rising costs in almost every aspect of their lives. By making health, life, and disability insurance more accessible, we can provide a layer of protection for those who need it most. In the context of a trade war with the US, addressing the affordability crisis through more affordable insurance could help buffer Canadian families from economic instability. If these households can rely on affordable insurance to protect themselves from life's inevitable setbacks, they will be in a better position to manage whatever external pressures come their way. It's about giving people the tools to recover when things go wrong, so they can continue to contribute to society and the economy without being completely wiped out by one misfortune.

Universal Or Subsidized Insurance Models

When it comes to addressing the affordability crisis, looking at universal or subsidized insurance models can offer a significant solution. These models help reduce the financial strain on individuals and families, particularly when it comes to healthcare. The idea behind universal or subsidized insurance is that everyone should have access to the essential coverage they need, without the fear of going bankrupt because of a medical emergency. It's a concept rooted in the belief that healthcare is a fundamental right, not a privilege for those who can afford it.

In Canada, we've seen the benefits of a single-payer system, where the government provides healthcare coverage to all residents, largely funded through taxes. This model ensures that people do not have to make the difficult decision between paying for medical care and other necessities like food or rent. The public system in Canada allows individuals to access care without worrying about out-of-pocket expenses, which is especially important for lower-income families. While the system is not without its challenges, the core benefit is that everyone, regardless of income, has access to essential healthcare services. This kind of model eliminates the need for families to take on expensive private insurance plans that may not even cover all of their healthcare needs.

In the US, we've seen a different approach with the Affordable Care Act (Obamacare), which aimed to make healthcare more accessible through subsidized insurance plans. The program was designed to provide coverage for people who might not be able to afford it otherwise. It works by offering subsidies to lower-income individuals and families, so they can purchase insurance through government-run exchanges. While not a universal system like Canada's, Obamacare has helped millions of Americans gain access to insurance who otherwise might have gone uninsured, especially those with pre-existing conditions. In many ways, Obamacare is a step toward universal coverage, offering a model for how the government can intervene to make healthcare more affordable for everyone.

The idea of universal or subsidized insurance systems isn't just about making healthcare more accessible; it's also about reducing the financial burden that illness can place on individuals and families. When people don't have to choose between paying for a doctor's visit and paying for groceries, they're less likely to fall into financial hardship. Universal insurance systems like Canada's or subsidized models like Obamacare also help to spread the costs of healthcare across the population, making it more affordable for everyone. In the long run, these systems can even reduce overall healthcare costs by focusing on prevention and early treatment rather than waiting until someone requires emergency care.

When thinking about how Canada can navigate a potential trade war with the US, these kinds of insurance models could play an important role. If healthcare is taken care of, it frees up resources for families to handle other challenges, whether it's paying for higher costs of living or dealing with the economic impact of a trade conflict. A universal or subsidized insurance system helps ensure that people are healthier, more financially stable, and better able to weather the economic storms that might come their way. In a time of economic uncertainty, having access to affordable healthcare provides a foundation that allows individuals to continue contributing to society without the added stress of looming medical costs.

Government Mandates And Employer Contributions

When thinking about how to make life more affordable for everyday Canadians, government mandates and employer contributions play a big role in ensuring that people are financially secure, especially when it comes to saving for retirement. One of the most important aspects of this is mandatory pension contributions, which are set up to help workers save for the future. Without these kinds of mandates, many people would struggle to put money aside, especially given how expensive life is becoming. The idea behind mandatory pension plans is to make saving for retirement not just a personal choice but a shared responsibility between the individual, the employer, and the government.

In Canada, we've seen how important these mandates can be through the Canada Pension Plan (CPP). Everyone who works contributes to CPP, and in return, they are guaranteed a pension when they retire, which helps reduce the risk of falling into poverty in old age. This system ensures that no one is left behind, even if they don't have the means or knowledge to save on their own. By mandating contributions, the government is essentially setting up a system of shared responsibility where both the public and private sectors work together to secure people's financial futures.

Employers also play a key role in this by making contributions on behalf of their employees. For many workers, especially those in low-wage or part-time jobs, employer contributions are often the only way they are able to save for retirement at all. These contributions add up over time, providing a more substantial nest egg than what an individual might be able to save on their own. It's a partnership where the employer and the government work together to make sure workers aren't left to fend for themselves when they retire. By ensuring that both sides are contributing, it makes it easier for people to save, even if they don't have much disposable income to set aside themselves.

This system helps to level the playing field, particularly for workers who might not have access to private retirement savings plans through their employer or who are unable to save on their own. The combination of mandatory government contributions and employer contributions creates a system of retirement savings that doesn't leave anyone behind. This is particularly important in times of economic uncertainty, like during a trade war, when job security and financial stability can become more difficult to achieve. Knowing that there is a reliable, mandated system to help people save for the future can provide a much-needed sense of security, and it also takes some of the pressure off individuals, freeing them to focus on other financial challenges.

By tackling affordability from this angle, Canada can help mitigate some of the negative impacts of external pressures like a trade war. When people aren't worried about how they'll make ends meet in retirement, they're better able to deal with the short-term challenges of rising living costs, unemployment, or economic instability. A strong, government-backed pension system is an essential tool in ensuring long-term financial security, and it helps Canadians weather the storm when things get tough.

Private Savings Programs And Employer Contributions

Private savings programs and employer contributions are crucial pieces of the puzzle when it comes to helping people save for retirement. A key example of this is tax-deferred savings accounts, like RRSPs (Registered Retirement Savings Plans) in Canada. These accounts allow people to set aside money for the future without having to pay taxes on that income until they withdraw it. This is a huge advantage because it gives people more freedom to save for the long-term, while also reducing their taxable income in the present. For someone trying to build a retirement nest egg, the ability to grow savings without immediately having to pay taxes can make a big difference over time.

Along with tax-deferred savings, employer-matched pension plans are another effective tool in encouraging retirement savings. These programs work by having employers match the contributions that employees make to their pension plans. So, for example, if an employee contributes a certain percentage of their salary to their pension, their employer will add an equal amount on top of that. This is essentially "free money," and it provides a powerful incentive for people to save more than they might otherwise be able to. Many people may not feel like they can afford to put much money into savings, but with an employer-matched plan, it becomes easier to build a larger retirement fund without having to sacrifice too much of their take-home pay.

The combination of private savings programs like RRSPs and employer contributions creates a system where saving for retirement becomes more accessible to more people. While there are still barriers for some individuals—such as low-income workers or those who are self-employed—these policies help many Canadians feel more confident about their financial futures. They also create an environment where individuals are encouraged to think long-term about their savings, which is critical when it comes to retirement planning. Rather than relying on the government alone to provide a safety net in old age, these policies give people the tools they need to be more financially independent and secure.

When people are able to save more effectively for retirement, they can better navigate the challenges that come with economic downturns, like a trade war with the US. In times of financial uncertainty, knowing that there is a solid retirement plan in place provides people with a sense of security, helping to reduce the overall pressure on public systems. The more people are able to save on their own, the less burden there is on government programs and services. This makes it easier for Canada to focus on addressing other issues, without having to rely too heavily on external factors like international trade agreements or foreign investments.

Ultimately, encouraging private savings through programs like RRSPs and employer-matched pensions gives Canadians the freedom and the tools to secure their financial future. This is an essential part of tackling the affordability crisis, as it helps people feel more in control of their finances and less reliant on external sources of income. It also ensures that people are able to weather difficult times, such as a trade war, with a little more confidence and stability.

Addressing The Retirement Savings Gap

The retirement savings gap in Canada is growing, and it's a serious issue that deserves more attention. The gap refers to the difference in retirement savings between different income groups, with lower-income workers often falling far behind their higher-income counterparts. This gap doesn't just affect people's ability to retire comfortably; it also creates long-term financial instability for families. Higher-income workers generally have access to employer-sponsored retirement plans, like pension programs, and they also have the disposable income to invest more in personal retirement savings. On the other hand, many lower-income workers are barely able to cover their day-to-day expenses, let alone put anything away for retirement. Without adequate retirement savings, they face the risk of financial insecurity when they can no longer work, which can place additional strain on government programs that were not designed to fully support retirees.

One of the primary reasons this gap exists is that low-income workers often don't have access to the same retirement savings programs that higher-income workers do. While some may have access to basic pension plans, many don't have the option of participating in employer-sponsored retirement savings programs that offer matching contributions. The situation is even worse for self-employed individuals who lack access to these kinds of programs altogether. As a result, lower-income Canadians are often left to rely on public pension programs like Old Age Security (OAS) and the Guaranteed Income Supplement (GIS), which, while valuable, are often not enough to maintain a decent standard of living in retirement. These programs are designed to provide a basic level of support, but they don't replace the kind of financial security that comes with personal retirement savings.

To address this growing gap, we need to make retirement savings more accessible to all Canadians, particularly those in low-income brackets. One potential solution is to expand access to retirement savings programs for low-income workers. Many low-income individuals are already eligible for some government-sponsored savings programs, such as the Canada Pension Plan (CPP), but these programs are still not enough on their own. One way to close the gap could be to offer a government-matched savings program specifically designed for low-income workers. The government could contribute a portion of the savings of lower-income earners, just as employers contribute to the retirement savings of higher-income employees. This would create a more level playing field and allow more people to build retirement savings without having to make significant sacrifices to their current financial situation.

Another idea is to make retirement savings programs more flexible for people with irregular or low incomes. Many low-income workers may face periods of unemployment or underemployment, which can make it difficult for them to contribute consistently to retirement savings. Providing more flexible options that allow workers to contribute at varying rates, based on their financial situation, could help bridge the gap. Additionally, making it easier for self-employed individuals to access retirement savings programs would give them the same opportunities as those in traditional employment.

Bridging the retirement savings gap is essential not only for the financial well-being of individuals but also for the broader economy. When more people have the means to save for retirement, they are less reliant on government programs and more able to sustain themselves. This creates a more stable economic environment and reduces the financial burden on public services. By addressing the growing gap in retirement savings, we can help Canadians weather economic challenges, including potential trade wars, with greater security and confidence. With the right policies in place, we can ensure that all Canadians have the ability to retire comfortably, regardless of their income level.

Taxation And Wealth Redistribution

Progressive taxation is one of the most effective tools we have for addressing the growing affordability crisis in Canada, especially as we prepare for the potential impacts of a trade war with the United States. Essentially, progressive taxes are taxes that increase with income, meaning that those who earn more pay a higher percentage of their income in taxes. This approach is rooted in the idea that those who are more financially secure should contribute more to the overall functioning of society, especially when it comes to funding essential services like healthcare, education, and infrastructure.

By implementing fair and progressive tax policies, we can ensure that wealth is redistributed in a way that helps to address affordability issues, particularly for lower-income households. In Canada, as in many other countries, the wealthiest individuals and corporations often pay a disproportionately small share of taxes relative to their income and wealth. This creates an environment where the richest members of society are able to accumulate even more wealth, while the rest of the population struggles to make ends meet. A fair tax policy that places a higher burden on the wealthiest individuals and corporations would allow the government to invest more in programs and services that directly benefit everyday Canadians, reducing the financial strain on low and middle-income families.

One of the ways in which progressive taxation can help alleviate affordability concerns is by funding social programs that provide direct support to those in need. With increased tax revenues, the government can expand access to healthcare, education, and housing, all of which are essential to improving quality of life. By investing in these areas, we can reduce the out-of-pocket costs that families face and ensure that basic needs are met, regardless of income. This is particularly important as we deal with rising costs in areas like healthcare and housing, where many Canadians are already feeling the pressure. Progressive taxation also enables the government to provide subsidies or benefits to low-income individuals and families, helping to lift them out of poverty and provide them with a safety net.

In addition to supporting social programs, progressive taxation can also help to reduce income inequality. The growing wealth gap in Canada is a significant issue, and a fair tax system can play a key role in narrowing that gap. By taxing the wealthiest Canadians at a higher rate, we can ensure that they contribute more to the country's prosperity, which can then be reinvested in communities that need it most. This helps create a more balanced society where everyone has access to the opportunities and resources they need to thrive. It's not just about redistributing wealth; it's about creating a more equitable society where the wealthiest members of society don't control an outsized share of the country's resources.

Of course, implementing progressive taxation isn't without its challenges. There are always debates about the right balance between encouraging economic growth and ensuring that the wealthy pay their fair share. However, if done correctly, progressive taxes can be a powerful tool for addressing affordability issues while fostering a more inclusive and sustainable economy. In the context of a trade war with the United States, where global economic pressures are at their highest, having a strong and fair tax system will allow Canada to weather those pressures and continue to provide for its citizens. A fair tax system, paired with investments in public services, can reduce the financial burdens on families, increase economic mobility, and help Canada maintain its competitive edge without resorting to protectionist measures or damaging trade conflicts.

In the end, progressive taxation isn't just about raising revenue; it's about making sure that everyone has a fair shot at success. By redistributing wealth in a way that addresses the needs of the most vulnerable in society, we can build a more equitable and resilient economy. This is crucial as we look ahead to potential challenges like a trade war with the US By ensuring that our tax policies are fair and equitable, we can help Canada navigate difficult economic times while protecting the financial well-being of all Canadians.

Social Assistance Expansion

One of the most impactful ways Canada can address the affordability crisis, especially as we prepare for challenges like a potential trade war with the United States, is by expanding welfare programs to include something like a Guaranteed Minimum Income (GMI). This type of program could replace existing structures like unemployment insurance, social assistance, and family benefits, creating a streamlined system that ensures every individual has access to the essentials, no matter their situation.

The idea behind a Guaranteed Minimum Income is simple but powerful. It guarantees a basic income to everyone, regardless of employment status or other factors, to ensure that they can meet their most basic needs. This could be a game-changer for Canadians who are living paycheck to paycheck, or who find themselves caught in the gaps of our current social safety net. By guaranteeing an income floor, we would remove the stigma and bureaucracy often associated with applying for and receiving assistance. Everyone, no matter their job situation, would know that they have a certain amount of income to rely on, ensuring that they can afford things like food, housing, healthcare, and other essentials.

One of the key advantages of a Guaranteed Minimum Income is its ability to simplify the social welfare system. Right now, the patchwork of programs like unemployment insurance, social assistance, and family benefits can be complex, and not everyone who needs help is able to access it easily. A GMI would replace these fragmented programs with a single, straightforward system that anyone who qualifies could use. It would eliminate a lot of the red tape that people face when trying to get help. More importantly, it would make sure that no one is left behind, regardless of whether they are currently employed, have children, or face other challenges.

A GMI also makes sense in the context of a trade war with the US If the economic landscape becomes more uncertain and jobs are lost, or industries struggle, having a guaranteed income would provide a cushion for Canadians. It would reduce the impact of job loss or economic downturns, helping people maintain their standard of living even during difficult times. This is crucial when facing external pressures, as it allows Canada to remain resilient in the face of economic upheaval. People would not be as vulnerable to the fluctuations of the job market or international trade policies if they had a basic income to rely on.

Additionally, the Guaranteed Minimum Income could address the issue of inequality, which is a significant challenge in Canada. Many people, especially those in lower-income brackets, struggle to make ends meet. The cost of living continues to rise, and wages have not kept up. With a GMI, we could ensure that the most vulnerable in our society have a stable foundation, preventing them from falling deeper into poverty. It would also help to reduce the reliance on temporary or unstable work, as individuals would not be forced to take any job simply to survive. Instead, they could make more thoughtful decisions about employment, retraining, or pursuing opportunities that align with their skills and interests, rather than just working to survive.

By implementing a Guaranteed Minimum Income, Canada would be able to provide security and dignity to its citizens. It's an investment in the well-being of everyone, especially those who are most at risk. This type of welfare state expansion would not only address the affordability crisis but would also ensure that we are ready for whatever economic challenges come our way, including a trade war. It would make our social safety net more effective, less stigmatized, and more universally accessible, making it a critical piece of the puzzle in building a fairer, more resilient society.

Economic Growth And Affordability

When we talk about addressing the affordability crisis, we can't overlook the role that government investment plays in creating long-term economic growth. A thriving economy doesn't just happen; it requires intentional efforts to build strong foundations that will support people for years to come. This is where the government can step in and make a significant difference by investing in areas like education, healthcare, and infrastructure. These investments not only make life more affordable in the short term but also contribute to sustainable growth that can weather the storm of any economic disruption, including a trade war with the United States.

Education is one of the most powerful tools for ensuring long-term affordability. When the government invests in education, it's not just about helping individuals learn the skills they need to enter the workforce. It's about creating a more skilled and adaptable workforce that can meet the demands of a rapidly changing economy. The more people are educated, the more likely they are to secure stable, well-paying jobs, which in turn helps to reduce financial stress on families. Education is also a great equalizer, providing opportunities for people from all backgrounds to succeed. By making education more accessible and affordable, the government can reduce income inequality, which plays a huge role in the affordability crisis.

Healthcare is another area where government investment is crucial. We know that healthcare is expensive, and many families are stretched thin trying to pay for it. The rising costs of insurance, medications, and medical procedures only add to the financial burden. But when the government steps in to ensure that healthcare is accessible and affordable, it takes a significant weight off people's shoulders. This is not just about emergency medical care, but also preventative care, which can reduce long-term costs by addressing health issues before they become more expensive to treat. A healthier population is a more productive population, and investing in healthcare now will pay dividends in the future, making it easier for Canadians to live without the constant worry of medical expenses.

Infrastructure is one of those areas that doesn't get as much attention as it should when we talk about affordability, but it's a game-changer. Roads, public transportation, energy grids, broadband; these are the things that help an economy run smoothly and keep costs down for everyone. By investing in infrastructure, the government can improve efficiency, reduce costs, and create jobs in the process. Take public transportation as an example. If more people can rely on affordable, accessible public transportation, they don't need to worry about the rising costs of owning a car, paying for gas, or dealing with maintenance. When infrastructure is modernized and expanded, it opens up new opportunities for people to work, live, and thrive without the constant pressure of rising transportation costs.

These kinds of investments don't just make life more affordable for individuals, they also contribute to a stronger economy. When people are healthier, better educated, and have access to reliable infrastructure, they are more productive. Businesses benefit because they have a more skilled and healthier workforce to rely on. The government can also create an environment where businesses can thrive by providing them with the tools they need to grow. This type of long-term growth benefits everyone and helps cushion the economy against shocks like trade wars or international instability. If we are able to grow the economy in a way that is sustainable, equitable, and rooted in investments that people can actually benefit from, we'll be better prepared to handle whatever comes our way, including the economic challenges that a trade war with the US might bring.

By focusing on these areas, the government can help drive economic growth in a way that makes life more affordable for everyone. These investments aren't just about immediate relief, but about setting up systems that will keep costs down and ensure that Canadians have the resources they need to succeed. In the long run, this approach can help Canada navigate the uncertainties of global trade and provide a solid foundation for growth, no matter what happens in the future.

Addressing The Hazard Of Economic Disruption Act

If Canada wants to prepare for the challenges of a trade war with the United States and tackle its affordability crisis at the same time, it needs more than ideas. It needs a practical framework to bring these ideas to life. That's where something like the "Addressing The Hazard Of Economic Disruption Act" could come into play. This is a barebones legislative blueprint that weaves together many of the strategies we've discussed. It's not about adding bells and whistles. It's about creating a clear, focused set of policies that target the root causes of affordability issues while safeguarding the economy from external shocks like trade disputes.

Economic Disription Affordability Acceleration Fund

In the event of an arduous economic disruption such as a pandemic or excessive tariffs imposed upon Canadian goods and services by a foreign government, additional funds will be allocated to all the economic measures in this act, in the same proportion that they are allocated by this act. For the first year this additional allocation will be [suggested value: eighty] billion dollars, and [suggested value: forty] billion dollars for every year afterwards, or as reallocated by parliament.

A Minimum Income Tax shall be paid, as required by this Act, on the income for each taxation year of every person resident in Canada at any time in the year and is liable for tax in the highest amount from the following calculations:

- The amount as determined by each person's income tax calculation according to Canadian law.
- 10% of each persons gross income, excluding Federal non-refundable tax credits.

Minimum Non-Profit Tax

Any non-profit that conducts business in Canada generating any form of revenue shall pay to Her Majesty in right of Canada the taxes for a taxation year and is liable for tax in the highest amount from the following calculations:

- 6.25% of each non-profit's net income.
- 1.75% of each non-profit's gross revenue.

Minimum Corporate Tax

Any corporation that conducts business in Canada generating any form of revenue shall pay to Her Majesty in right of Canada the taxes for a taxation year and is liable for tax in the highest amount from the following calculations:

- The amount as determined by each corporation's tax calculation according to Canadian law.
- A percentage of each corporation's net income equal to half their net tax rate.
- 3.5% of each corporation's gross revenue.

Canadian Essentials Of Life Tax (CEOLT)

Certain property and services supplied in or imported into Canada are subject to the Canadian Essentials Of Life Tax (CEOLT).

The items below are categories of taxable supplies:

- housing rentals and leasing
- electricity, heating fuels, water delivery, waste and sewer services
- physical and mental healthcare services, including dental and pharmacy
- assisted living and medical devices
- insurance services
- automobile and passenger vehicle sales
- grocery sales
- clothing and footwear sales
- telecommunication services
- cable and streaming services

Canadian Essentials Of Life Tax Rate

Any person or corporation that conducts business in Canada that derive at least 25% of their gross revenue for the year in Canada from the sale of taxable supplies (10% for basic groceries) is liable for tax equal to 30% of each corporation's gross revenue.

Tax Reduction For Canadian Persons

A Canadian person benefits from a 10% reduction of the CEOLT.

Tax Reduction For Canadian-Controlled Private Corporations (CCPCs)

A CCPC benefit from a 10% reduction of the CEOLT.

Tax Reduction For Meating The Tax Abatement Requirements

Any person or corporation that meats the minimum tax abatement requirements for each category of taxable supplies that they sell benefits from a 10% reduction to their CEOLT taxation rate, and meeting the maximum tax abatement requirements for each category of taxable supplies that they sell benefits from a 20% reduction to their CEOLT taxation rate.

Canada Revenue Agency And Tax Abatement Requirements

The determination of tax abatement requirements by various entities will use systems as created by the CRA to minimize the burden imposed on the CRA to implement the Canadian Essentials Of Life Tax.

Tax Abatement Requirements For Various Categories

From time to time, parliament will designate the appropriate the appropriate authority to determine the specific values (including limits) for the minimum and maximum tax abatement requirements for each category.

Tax Abatement Requirements For Housing (Example)

Where all their units are adequately maintained and do not exceed the market rental rate for each unit type for their area, a landlord qualifies for the minimum tax abatement for the housing category. Landlords that also maintain at least 15% of their housing units as affordable housing (as determined by their regional authority) qualify for the maximum tax abatement.

Tax Abatement Requirements For Grocery (Example)

A grocery supplier that universally offers at least a 15% discount on grocery sales to low-income persons qualifies for the minimum tax abatement for the grocery category. A grocery supplier that universally offers at least a 25% discount on grocery sales to impoverished persons qualifies for the maximum tax abatement for the grocery category.

Guaranteed Minimum Income (GMI)

The Guaranteed Minimum Income program is established as a federal initiative to ensure every Canadian has access to financial resources that cover basic necessities, including shelter, food, and utilities. The program is universal, replacing the current employment insurance system, and is funded through payroll contributions from employees and employers, as well as general government revenues.

Payroll Contributions

To fund the GMI, all employed individuals contribute 3% of their gross income through payroll deductions. Employers are required to match this contribution at a reduced rate of 1.5% of the employee's gross income. These funds are collected by the Canada Revenue Agency and allocated to a dedicated GMI fund to ensure transparency and accountability.

Eligibility and Payments

All Canadian citizens and permanent residents over the age of 18 are eligible for the GMI, regardless of employment status. Payments are calculated based on a standardized formula that prioritizes covering the cost of basic necessities. The amount an individual receives is determined by their income level, household size, and regional cost of living. The maximum GMI payment will be set according to the government's financial capacity, ensuring it does not impose an unreasonable burden on the national budget.

Income Adjustments and Caps

GMI payments decrease incrementally as an individual's income increases, creating a graduated system that supports those most in need while maintaining an incentive to work. For households with higher incomes, GMI payments phase out entirely once their income exceeds a predetermined threshold. This ensures resources are directed where they are needed most.

Integration with Existing Benefits

GMI will replace employment insurance entirely, streamlining the system to reduce administrative costs and duplication. It will also be integrated with other federal and provincial benefits, such as housing subsidies and child benefits, to avoid redundancy and improve efficiency. Recipients of GMI will not face clawbacks on other benefits, ensuring comprehensive support.

Fiscal Responsibility and Review

To maintain fiscal responsibility, the GMI program will be subject to annual review by an independent body. This body will assess the program's impact on poverty reduction, workforce participation, and government finances. Adjustments to payment levels, eligibility criteria, or payroll contribution rates may be made to align with Canada's economic conditions and budgetary constraints.

Implementation Timeline

The program will be rolled out over five years, starting with pilot projects in selected regions to refine its structure and address potential challenges. A gradual phase-in ensures employers, employees, and government systems can adapt to the new framework without disruption.

Transparency and Public Reporting

A public reporting system will provide Canadians with regular updates on the program's performance, including its impact on reducing poverty and improving financial security. Clear communication with the public is essential for building trust and ensuring the program's long-term success.

Canadian National Affordable Housing Co-operative (CNAHC)

The Affordable Housing Fund and the Apartment Construction Loan Program will be phased out and replaced by the Canadian National Affordable Housing Co-operative (CNAHC), a new crown corporation fully funded by the federal government with an annual budget of [suggested value: ten] billion dollars. The CNAHC will operate on a cooperative model, ensuring that all tenants are members with a stake in the organization. The primary goal of the CNAHC will be to build large multi-unit rental properties, with each property containing 100 or more units. These developments will be designed to meet the needs of low- and moderate-income Canadians, providing affordable and stable housing options in communities across the country. By using a cooperative model, the CNAHC will foster a sense of ownership and involvement among tenants, allowing them to have a direct say in how their housing is managed. This approach will ensure that housing remains affordable, secure, and supportive of the long-term needs of its members.

The National Accessible and Safe Unsheltered Services Agency (NASUSA)

The National Accessible and Safe Unsheltered Services Agency (NASUSA) will be established as a federal program to address the growing issue of tent cities in urban areas across Canada. This agency will acquire large properties in cities that are struggling with unsheltered populations, providing safe spaces and essential services for individuals living in temporary or portable shelters such as tents. NASUSA's mission will be to create secure, accessible environments where unsheltered individuals can have a dignified living situation with the necessary resources to meet their basic needs.

The agency will offer a range of services designed specifically for tent city living, which may include a combination of free and paid services. These services will include security measures to ensure the safety of all residents, management of community rules to maintain order and foster positive relationships, and utility services that are tailored to the specific needs of tent-based living. NASUSA will also provide shared facilities for cooking, recreation, and hygiene, including communal kitchens, recreational areas, and bathroom and shower facilities. Additionally, each resident will have access to a mailbox for personal mail and small secure storage areas, such as lockers, to keep their belongings safe.

To ensure a peaceful and supportive environment, clients will be required to follow specific rules and guidelines. These rules will include prohibitions on drugs and illegal conduct, as well as expectations for good community behavior. NASUSA will also collaborate with government agencies at all levels and nonprofit organizations that work with unsheltered populations, offering space for these partners to provide vital services to individuals in need. By offering these services, NASUSA aims to create stable and supportive living conditions for unsheltered individuals while helping to address the challenges faced by tent city communities across the country.

NASUSA Store

In addition to its core services, the National Accessible and Safe Unsheltered Services Agency (NASUSA) will establish the NASUSA Store, a not-for-profit space dedicated to providing clients with access to affordable essentials. The NASUSA Store will sell items such as food, hygiene products, clothing, and other necessities at reasonable prices, ensuring clients can access what they need to maintain their dignity and quality of life.

The store will also play a pivotal role in supporting clients who are ready to transition to more stable living conditions. Using the profits generated from sales, the NASUSA Store will fund a financing program for working clients, enabling them to purchase semi-permanent housing options like yurts or tiny homes. These structures will serve as a critical step up from tents, offering more stability and comfort while remaining accessible to those with limited resources. Clients participating in the financing program will receive support in navigating the process, ensuring the opportunity is both manageable and empowering.

By incorporating the NASUSA Store into its operations, the agency not only addresses immediate needs but also provides a pathway for clients to achieve greater housing security. This initiative reflects NASUSA's commitment to creating practical, long-term solutions for unsheltered individuals while fostering independence and dignity.

NASUSA And Sex Workers

A safe sex workers program is essential for ensuring the success of initiatives like NASUSA while addressing the vulnerabilities of women among homeless and unhoused populations. Many women in these circumstances turn to sex work out of necessity, often in unsafe and exploitative environments. A structured program could provide them with access to safe working conditions, health services, and legal protections, empowering them to make choices without fear of violence or coercion. By prioritizing their safety and rights, the program would also reduce the stigma surrounding sex work, allowing for better support and outreach. Connecting these women to housing and social services would create a bridge to stability, ensuring they are not left behind in broader efforts to address homelessness. Programs like these reinforce the idea that everyone, regardless of their circumstances or choices, deserves dignity and safety in their daily lives.

The Protection and Safety of Sex Workers Program

The Protection and Safety of Sex Workers program is introduced to create a framework that ensures the dignity, safety, and well-being of individuals engaged in legal sex work. This legislation is grounded in respect for human rights and acknowledges sex work as legitimate labor, deserving of the same protections as any other profession.

Legal Recognition and Employment Rights

Sex work is recognized as a lawful profession under this act, granting workers the same legal rights and protections as those in other industries. Sex workers are entitled to employment contracts, fair wages, and access to benefits such as healthcare, insurance, and retirement savings plans. Employers in the sex industry are required to adhere to labor laws, including providing safe working environments and protecting workers from exploitation.

Workplace Safety Standards

To ensure safety, all establishments where sex work occurs must meet strict workplace health and safety standards. This includes well-lit and secure premises, panic buttons or other emergency measures, and access to private spaces for workers to rest. Workers must be provided with personal protective equipment, where applicable, and regular health check-ups facilitated without stigma or coercion.

Protection from Exploitation and Coercion

The act criminalizes any form of coercion, trafficking, or exploitation within the sex industry. Employers and managers who engage in these practices face severe penalties, including imprisonment and heavy fines. A dedicated task force will be established to monitor and investigate reports of abuse or exploitation, with anonymous reporting mechanisms available for workers.

Access to Legal and Health Services

Sex workers are guaranteed access to legal aid, healthcare services, and counseling without fear of discrimination. Healthcare providers are required to offer services in a nonjudgmental and confidential manner, covering sexual and mental health needs. Legal clinics will provide free consultations to assist workers with contracts, disputes, or other legal matters related to their profession.

Anti-Stigma Campaigns and Public Awareness

The government will fund public education campaigns aimed at reducing stigma associated with sex work. These campaigns will promote understanding and respect, encouraging society to view sex work as legitimate employment. Educational programs will also be offered to law enforcement and healthcare providers to improve their interactions with sex workers.

License and Registration Requirements

Establishments operating within the sex industry must obtain licenses and comply with rigorous registration requirements. This ensures accountability and creates a transparent system where workers' rights are protected. Independent workers have the option to register for legal recognition, granting them access to benefits without forcing unnecessary oversight.

Support for Transition and Exit Programs

Recognizing that not all sex workers wish to remain in the industry indefinitely, the act funds programs to support those who wish to transition to other forms of employment. These programs include skills training, job placement services, and financial assistance to help workers establish themselves in new careers.

Law Enforcement Guidelines

Law enforcement agencies are prohibited from targeting or harassing sex workers who operate within the bounds of the law. Police are trained to focus on protecting workers from violence, exploitation, and abuse rather than criminalizing their profession. Specialized units will be established to respond to incidents involving sex workers, ensuring their safety and dignity are prioritized.

Monitoring and Evaluation

A national board will oversee the implementation of this act, regularly reviewing its effectiveness in improving safety and working conditions. The board will consult with sex workers and industry stakeholders to ensure the law evolves in line with their needs.

Expanding The Barebones Legislative Framework

The barebones legislative framework of the 'Addressing The Hazard Of Economic Disruption Act' is designed to be a starting point, not a finished product. Its purpose is to give legislators a solid foundation to build on, allowing for expansion and refinement as needed. This approach recognizes that no single policy can address the affordability crisis on its own. Instead, the act is meant to serve as a central hub where all of Canada's affordability programs can be consolidated and streamlined.

By combining programs like housing assistance, public transportation investment, healthcare affordability, and retirement savings support under one legislative umbrella, we create an integrated system that addresses the real, everyday concerns of Canadians. This also allows for better coordination between federal and provincial efforts, ensuring resources are used efficiently and effectively.

The act emphasizes flexibility, enabling lawmakers to adapt it to the diverse needs of different communities. Rural areas, for instance, might require more emphasis on transportation solutions and regional economic development, while urban centers could focus on housing affordability and reducing living costs. By building this adaptability into the legislative design, the act can be tailored to tackle unique challenges without losing sight of its overarching goal.

The blueprint encourages lawmakers to include meaningful policies like a guaranteed minimum income, universal childcare, and investments in green infrastructure, all of which directly improve affordability. It also leaves room for addressing gaps in existing systems, ensuring that no Canadian is left behind. This collaborative and expandable approach makes it possible to craft solutions that matter to everyone, from single parents in cities to seniors in remote communities.

This act is not just about programs or policies; it's about creating a framework where the conversation around affordability becomes proactive and comprehensive. It gives legislators the tools they need to turn ideas into action, ensuring that every piece of the puzzle fits into a bigger picture of economic stability and fairness. It's a way of saying to Canadians that their needs are not just acknowledged but prioritized.